NAPERVILLE
Reflections of Community

NAPERVILLE
Reflections of Community

•

Text by Jini Leeds Clare

Photographs by Brian Lewis

•

SPONSORS

Naperville Area Chamber of Commerce
City of Naperville
The Naperville Development Partnership
The Amoco Research Center in Naperville
Ameritech
W. Brand Bobosky
Crestview Builders
First Chicago
Harris Bank Naperville
MidAmerica Federal
Prostaff
Standard Federal Bank
Toenniges Jewelers
Wegner Plumbing Company
Edward Health Services Corporation
Central DuPage Health System
Glen Ellyn Clinic
Copley Memorial Hospital
Saint Joseph Medical Center
North Central College
Benedictine University
College of DuPage
DePaul University
Naperville's School Districts
Holiday Inn Select
Naper Settlement
Naperville Park District
Naperville Township
Naperville Visitors Bureau

ACKNOWLEDGMENTS

Layout, design, and production of this publication by Platinum Publishing Company, Inc.
7 Old Solomon's Island Road
Annapolis, Maryland 21401
(410) 224-1111/(800) 783-1238

Text ©1997 by Jini Leeds Clare.
Photographs ©1997 by Brian Lewis.

Platinum would like to thank the entire membership for its overwhelming support of the Naperville Area Chamber of Commerce and this book. It is through your support that the Naperville Area Chamber of Commerce continues to grow and prosper.
Platinum also recognizes the staff of the Naperville Area Chamber of Commerce. Their patience and hard work have made this publication a success.
The information in this book has been provided to Platinum and the Naperville Area Chamber of Commerce, and therefore cannot be assumed correct or free from error. Platinum and the Naperville Area Chamber of Commerce assume no responsibility for the accuracy of information contained herein.

1st Printing, 1997.

ISBN 1-890291-03-X

Color separation and film preparation by Platinum Publishing Company, Inc.

This is NAPER

Walk across a covered bridge and listen to the rushing water below. Stop and admire the lilacs, and discover the pointed stump a beaver has gnawed along the banks of the Riverwalk. Listen to the laughter of children as they play soccer in a field of grass, and watch their younger brothers and sisters attempting somersaults along the sidelines. Witness the joy at the community center as a group of retired men and women plan an upcoming trip, and smell the wonderful aroma of home-cooked meals volunteers will soon deliver to elderly who live alone.

This is Naperville.

Drive along the tollway and count the major research centers that place the city on the leading edge of technology. Then saunter along Jefferson Avenue in Naperville's charming downtown. Glance through the windows of an old-fashioned meat market, a family-owned jewelry store, and a brimming antique shop. Spend the rest of your morning chatting with costumed guides at the historic Naper Settlement, then join your friends for lunch at a sidewalk cafe.

This is Naperville.

Another day, visit the school nearest your home and feel the respect the classroom teacher has for the students. Listen to the well-presented lesson, and observe the excitement in the children's eyes. Then, pick up the paper and read about the community fund-raiser to help a family in need.

This, too, is Naperville ...

A COMMUNITY OF CARING AND COMMERCE.

HISTO

THE RIVER'S SOURCE
Naperville's History

At first there was the river, a meandering stream that swelled from its banks whenever raindrops soaked the earth. The ground itself was like a sponge, with thick prairie grasses grasping the moisture, and underlying deposits of clay keeping it from seeping away.

Abundant wetlands stretched for miles. Crystal clear water moved silently, slowly— often in hidden channels— nourishing the roots of marsh vegetation. Drier prairies made up a quarter of the land. Tall native grasses undulated in the breezes, creating what appeared to be waves in vast oceans of green, white, purple or amber, depending on the season of the year. Woods, knolls and oak-laced savannas, filled with wildflowers and fire-resistant plants, dotted the landscape.

The richness of the land was a source of life for animals. Deer, elk, fox, mountain lion, coyote, bear, buffalo, muskrat, beaver, and raccoon all flourished in this habitat. So did a multitude of waterfowl and other wetland creatures.

The Illiniwek, and later the Miami, Iroquois, Sak, Fox, Kickapoo, and Pottawatomi, roamed throughout the area, hunting game, gathering nuts and berries, and planting corn and squash. They canoed the rivers, wandered dry river beds, and established a system of trails that were later to become important roads throughout the county. These Native Americans tamed the wilderness through fire, burning the tall prairie grasses to create clearings, encourage the growth of young berry-producing shrubs, and drive game toward waiting bows and arrows.

But other forces could not be tamed. In 1673, Father Jacques Marquette and French explorer Louis Joliet entered the region. They followed the Illinois and DesPlaines rivers from the Mississippi, portaged to the Chicago River, and went on to Lake Michigan, opening the territory to further exploration and, eventually, to extensive settlement.

Throughout the 1700s and early 1800s, trappers and traders traversed the area, reaping a bounty of valuable animal pelts. Locally, the best known of these traders was a Frenchman named DuPage. In 1800, he settled where the east and west branches of a river joined together — a river later named in his honor. According to local historian Genevieve Towsley in her book, *A View of Historic Naperville,* DuPage built a trading post at that site and traded wares with the Pottawatomi and Kickapoo Indians.

17

The first settlers were members of the Stephen Scott family, attracted to the area by the DuPage River. Stephen Scott and his son, Willard, discovered the river while on a hunting trip in August of 1830. They followed the waterway upstream until it split into two branches, in what is now Will County. The men decided to make this area their new home. In the fall, they returned with their families to build a cabin and establish a farm. By historical accounts, the Native Americans and Scott family lived in harmony.

In the spring of 1831, the Bailey Hobson family became the first pioneers to settle in DuPage County. They built a home along the west branch of the river, three miles north of the Scott family homestead, near what is now Hobson Road. The Hobsons later built a grist mill which drew people from miles around for flour and meal.

In July of 1831, Captain Joseph Naper, his wife Almeda, his brother John, and their families also journeyed to this area to begin a new life along the banks of the DuPage River. A permanent new settlement began to grow as the pioneers built their homes and several commercial ventures on land that is now part of downtown Naperville. Together, according to Towsley, the brothers built a trading house and conducted business with the settlers and the Pottawatomi Indians. By fall, they had built a log cabin school and hired a teacher for area youngsters. By the spring of 1832, the brothers had built a saw mill along the river at Mill Street, as well as a crude grist mill.

"Spirit of 1831" by Les Schrader.

Captain Joseph Naper and his fellow settlers set out on a three-day journey from Chicago to his land claim along the DuPage River which would become Naperville.

Fort Payne, Naper Settlement.

These early settlers were only a few of the thousands who ventured westward from New England, Ohio, Indiana, and Europe in search of land and opportunity. The rapid settlement of this region by the pioneers had a devastating effect on the Native Americans who had lived here for hundreds of years. In 1832, the Black Hawk War symbolized the struggles of the native peoples and dramatically affected life in Naper's settlement.

Pottawatomi Chief Aptakisic, known by the settlers as Chief Half Day, rode at night to the home of the Blodgett family where he had been a frequent visitor and urged that all the settlement families flee to Fort Dearborn in Chicago.

On May 18, most of the settlers left by wagon train, while groups of Pottawatomis continued to look out for the pioneers who remained behind.

Captain Naper and other settlers asked for military assistance to build a fort at the settlement. The request was granted, and Fort Payne was built on a hill overlooking the village, near where North Central College's Merner Field House is today.

In 1833, another treaty was signed, opening the remaining lands for settlement. Within three years, most of the native peoples had been removed from the area.

"Chief Half Day" by Les Schrader.

Pottawatomi Chief Half Day says goodbye to Naperville settlers after escorting them to Fort Dearborn in Chicago during the Black Hawk War of 1832.

"The Pre-Emption House" by Les Schrader.

Young Abraham Lincoln delivers a speech to a small crowd from the roof of the Pre-Emption House. Although Mr. Lincoln did not stop here on one of his documented speaking circuits, it is very likely he traveled through town to visit friends and clients. Oral history tradition states he made an impromptu speech on one of these visits.

After the Black Hawk War, the settlement continued to grow steadily. According to the historian Genevieve Towsley, by 1835 it "was a thriving village, located at the junction of two 'highways'" — one the stage route between Chicago and the booming Mississippi River town of Galena, and the other leading from Chicago to Ottawa and the state capital in Vandalia. The settlement's location at the crossroads helped the local economy and led to the construction of the county's first inn and tavern, the Pre-Emption House. It was a convenient stopping point for suppliers and travelers, a day's ride from Chicago. The river played an important part in the economy, too, with sawmills and grist mills providing the lumber and flour needed by the settlers. By 1839, DuPage County was established, and Naperville was selected as the county seat, a title the village later lost to Wheaton. Three years later, Joseph Naper surveyed and laid out the streets of the town. Then, in 1864, the Chicago, Burlington and Quincy Railroad laid its tracks through town, guaranteeing Naperville an important role in the area's commerce.

2 5

A replica of the original Pre-Emption House now stands on the grounds of Naper Settlement.

In the early days of the settlement, tall prairie grasses, root-laced sod, and wetlands made plowing extremely difficult. But the mass production of a lightweight steel plow in the late 1830s allowed farmers to cut through the sod, and tiling of the fields drained away unwanted water. The newly plowed soil was rich and fertile, and the area quickly became an important dairy farming region.

Business and industry flourished as well. By the turn of the century, Naperville was known for its retail shops, brick and tile works, plow factory, tree and shrub nurseries, cheese factory, and furniture and cigar manufacturing. Stone from Naperville's quarries was used to rebuild Chicago after the Great Chicago Fire, and it is said that Adolf Coors learned many of his brewing skills at Naperville's Stenger Brewery before he moved on to Golden, Colorado.

In 1931, residents donated time and money to celebrate the city's 100th anniversary with the purchase and dedication of Centennial Beach. This project has had a lasting effect on the quality of life in the community. The old quarry and property, located next to the DuPage River on the site of Naper's grist mill, became Naperville's public swimming facility and gathering place. Later it also became the centerpiece for the picturesque Riverwalk, the charming linear park that brings residents together and links them with the city's past.

Stenger Brewery.

A LARGE MUSHROOM PLANT
APERVILLE. ILLINOIS

Naperville's population began to grow following World War II as returning veterans took advantage of the GI Bill to attend college or purchase homes. The construction of the East-West Tollway, I-88, gave an even stronger boost to the local economy. Routed along the northern edge of Naperville, the highway provided faster travel to downtown Chicago. Major corporations, including AT&T Bell Laboratories and Amoco Research Center, moved to Naperville, building research and development facilities here.

Naperville soon became one of the fastest growing cities in the nation. The city's population almost doubled every decade from 1960 to 1990, growing from 13,000 residents to more than 85,000. A special census in 1996 put the population at more than 110,000 with projections that Naperville will have 135,000 residents by the year 2005.

Naperville is growing by leaps and bounds, and its high number of triplet births has received national attention.

30

QUALITY

O F L I F E

QUALITY OF LIFE
Flowing from Pride and Generosity

Just like Joseph Naper and the early settlers, today's community leaders have done an exceptional job of planning for the future and maintaining an outstanding quality of life. Strong intergovernmental cooperation helps the city, park district, forest preserve district and schools work together to provide excellent services — and a deep sense of pride unites the people of Naperville as they strive to make this a special, caring community for their families, friends, and newcomers.

In the schools, parents, teachers, community members, and businesses work together to enrich the curriculum and provide top educational experiences for the youth. The schools are among the finest in the nation, and students score well above national norms. The parks are beautiful and abundant, with more than 112 neighborhood and community parks for everyone to enjoy. Recreational activities are almost unlimited for every member of the family. Housing choices are varied with apartments, condos, historic homes, and new subdivisions to suit any lifestyle. Nearby hospitals and doctors provide excellent medical care, and the wealth of boutiques and larger malls creates a shopper's paradise. And efficient city government guarantees that emergencies will be handled quickly, growth will be managed carefully, and residents will receive the services they need.

But the quality of life in Naperville extends beyond housing, shopping, medical care, and the services residents receive from public agencies. It also comes from the generosity of the people and their concern for others. Community events that raise funds to build playgrounds, help abused children and fight homelessness bind Naperville's residents together. Whether volunteering to work at Ribfest, attending The Last Fling, or purchasing items at the Little Friends Auction, residents are continually making Naperville an even better place to live.

EDUCATION
Channeling Our Children's Potential

Naperville is served by two excellent public school districts, Naperville Community Unit School District 203 and Indian Prairie Community Unit School District 204, one of the fastest-growing districts in the state. The schools offer programs for students of all ability levels and provide a wealth of extracurricular activities for youth to enjoy. Student test scores on standardized tests are well above state and national averages. Highly skilled and dedicated teachers provide quality instruction, while parents and community volunteers support the schools with time and talent. Local businesses are actively involved with the schools through innovative and valuable partnerships.

Dozens of local scholars become National Merit Finalists each year, going on to excel at some of the greatest universities in the nation. Through team and individual efforts in math, business, applied technology, engineering, science, writing, spelling, vocational, and other curriculum-related areas, students achieve state or national recognition annually. Interscholastic athletic teams in badminton, baseball, basketball, cross country, football, golf, gymnastics, soccer, softball, swimming, tennis, track and field, volleyball, and wrestling regularly capture high state rankings. The schools also have strong cultural programs. Young thespians delight audiences with their productions throughout the year. Student musicians impress listeners with their choral, classical and jazz concerts. High school music organizations have been invited to perform at state, national, and international events. One local high school marching band has even performed in London, England, at the request of the Lord Mayor of Westminster.

A number of outstanding private schools are also located in the area. Bethany Lutheran School, Calvary Christian School, Sts. Peter and Paul Catholic School, and St. Raphael Catholic School in Naperville provide youngsters with Christian education, as does Benet Academy in nearby Lisle. The Illinois Math and Science Academy, a special facility for gifted math and science students throughout the state, is located in nearby Aurora.

Lee Marek, a teacher at Naperville North High School, and his "weird science" have appeared on "The Late Show with David Letterman."

Planetarium, Waubonsie Valley High School.

Naperville Community Unit School District 203

.Naperville District 203 is committed to the future of its students. That's why technology is embedded in most aspects of the curriculum, and in some cases technology leads to new and exciting teaching opportunities. Distance learning has allowed students to access people from around the world. Through video conferencing, students have chatted with politicians, compared notes with students throughout the country and even learned Japanese from a state university. The ever-changing and ever-growing Internet has also been a part of the curriculum for several years, giving students easy and safe access to the world.

Business education partnerships have broadened the students' worlds even further. Cooperation with local businesses of all sizes has allowed students to experience nature in a unique way, to test their physical and mental abilities on a climbing wall and to test their talents by producing work that has brought them peer recognition.

While partnerships with community groups have taught students social responsibility. A prime example is the teaming of Washington Junior High School, Harris Bank Naperville and CHILDSERV Emergency Group Home to help a group of abused or abandoned teenage girls. The schools also work with the Naperville Police Department on a reading program to build self-esteem and rapport with law enforcement officers.

Indian Prairie Community Unit School District 204

District 204 has found a unique way to work the Internet into its curriculum at every grade level. The district's "Virtual Museum" features teacher-selected World Wide Web sites - downloaded to the district's intranet - that relate to all subjects, including social studies and science. Students throughout the district can access these sites, as well as appropriate sites on the Internet, as part of their studies.

Using technology for learning is not new to District 204. In 1975, Waubonsie Valley High School was constructed with a planetarium, a rare and wonderful resource for students. The district has also built fully operational television studios into both high schools and has engaged in distance learning.

Unique partnerships with business also set District 204 apart. MidAmerica Federal Savings Bank, a local financial institution, and Waubonsie Valley High School have been recognized for the creation of the student-run Green and Gold Bank, a fully licensed facility which opened in 1995 in the school cafeteria. Students are trained in banking and work under the direction of a branch supervisor. Together, they provide savings bond and checking accounts, as well as bond, money order, and loan application services for students and faculty during the school day. High school teachers and bank personnel have also developed a two-year program of courses to help juniors and seniors prepare for banking careers, including finance, advertising, marketing, and general business.

Greenhouse, Indian Prairie District 204.

Green and Gold Bank, Waubonsie Valley High School.

3 9

Climbing Wall, Highlands Elementary School.

HIGHER EDUCATION
Providing a Bridge to the Future

Because the people of Naperville value quality education, and because of the city's proximity to the research and development corridor, Naperville has become a magnet for excellent colleges and universities. North Central College has played an influential role in the community since the school was located here in 1870. Benedictine University, founded by Benedictine monks as St. Procopius College, was established in nearby Lisle in 1887. More recently, the College of DuPage, DePaul University, Robert Morris College, and Loyola University have established branches in Naperville, and numerous other colleges have opened their doors nearby.

North Central College

For more than 125 years, North Central College has been an important educational, cultural, and economic anchor in Naperville's downtown. The college has provided training for local business leaders and educators, attracted high-caliber students from across the nation, and offered quality educational opportunities for residents.

With an enrollment of more than 2,600 students, the college offers a rich curriculum in liberal arts and sciences. In fact, North Central College has been ranked as one of "America's Best Colleges" by *U.S. News and World Report.*

In keeping with its significant role in the community, North Central College has begun work to link the campus to the Riverwalk . In doing so, the college will further strengthen a vibrant downtown.

"Old Main," North Central College.

College of DuPage Naperville Center.

Benedictine University.

Nichols Library.

NAPERVILLE PUBLIC LIBRARIES
Holding a Pool of Knowledge

Like many aspects of Naperville, the library holds a rich history too. Nichols Library was originally opened in 1895 and expanded in 1986. A second library was opened in the south end of town.

Children delight in their own special sections at each facility. Many youngsters enjoy popular storytimes and thousands of elementary-age children participate in the annual Summer Reading Program. Teens make heavy use of the libraries' resources to complete homework or check out the newest CDs, and adults utilize the library for recreational reading, business publications, research, and community presentations. For many residents, Naperville's public libraries are opening doors to high technology, with computers and modems allowing access to library information from home and research via CD-ROM.

NAPERVILLE HEALTH CARE
Providing a Fountain of Health

Naperville residents of all ages can be assured that excellent medical resources are available nearby. From neonatal units for at-risk newborns to tender services for elderly parents with Alzheimers, local facilities provide skilled and compassionate care.

Edward Hospital, located in the center of town, offers 24-hour emergency care, a high level trauma center, and numerous other medical services, including The Edward Cardiovascular Institute, The Women's Center for Health, and Edward Fitness Center. Just south of Edward Hospital's campus is Linden Oaks Hospital, an 84-bed psychiatric facility that provides treatment for anyone needing help with emotional, behavioral, or substance abuse problems.

Several other fine hospitals are located in nearby communities, including Central DuPage Hospital in Winfield, Rush-Copley Memorial Hospital in Aurora, and Good Samaritan Hospital in Downers Grove.

Naperville's emphasis on health is reflected each day by numerous wellness-in-the-workplace initiatives, by the large number of fitness centers in the area, and by the sidewalks filled with early morning joggers all over town. Local health care providers also offer community education programs, including CPR, coping skills, pre-natal classes, nutrition and support groups.

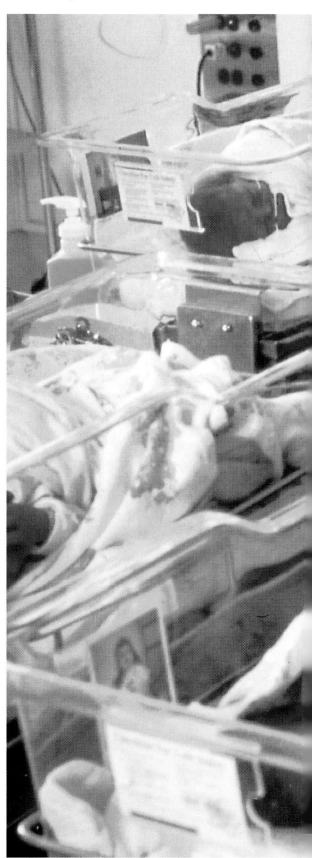

4 5

WORSHIP
Reflecting All Faiths

The spires of Sts. Peter and Paul Church in the heart of Naperville symbolize a community in which religion has always played a central role.

In the early days of the settlement, immigrants from New England, Alsace-Lorraine, and Germany brought a variety of rich religious traditions with them and quickly established congregations in Naperville. A few of the old churches stand as landmarks today, including Century Memorial Chapel at Naper Settlement, originally St. John's Episcopal Church.

Sts. Peter and Paul Church, one of the area's oldest churches.

47

Historically the German Evangelical Church, this building now holds the Naperville Woman's Club.

Today's churches reflect the diversity of a community that is growing ever more cosmopolitan. Worshippers of all faiths and cultures can find a church, synagogue, mosque or temple in Naperville or within a short drive of the community.

Many local families are involved in church activities that reach out to others. Whether serving food together at an area homeless shelter, collecting canned goods for local food pantries, or repairing homes for the needy in Appalachia, Naperville families spend memorable time together, living their beliefs.

49

Congregation Beth Shalom.

NAPERVILLE'S HOUSING
Surging with Choices

Until 50 years ago, Naperville was primarily a farming community. Remnants of those farmsteads can be seen today. However, with the rapid growth of Chicago's suburban population into Naperville, most of those old farms have been developed, one by one, into subdivisions.

Naperville has more than 285 subdivisions, earning it the friendly nickname "Neighborville." These subdivisions offer a wide variety of housing choices, from modern apartments and historic dwellings, to cozy center-hall colonials and spacious executive homes.

In a partnership that reflects a true sense of community, five times each year the presidents of each of Naperville's 100 or so homeowners' associations meet with city officials. In these Homeowners Confederation meetings, subdivision

representatives express their concerns about city services to the mayor, council members, and department heads. The homeowners receive direct answers to their questions and quick responses to their concerns. These meetings also encourage residents to share information with one another, uniting all geographic areas of the town.

A number of years ago, Naperville led the nation with the passage of a land-cash donations ordinance. It required developers to donate land or cash for the construction of parks and schools in each development. Because of this community vision, every local family has easy access to a friendly neighborhood park. Children have safe places to play near their homes, and neighbors have convenient places to gather for annual picnics, and other outings.

RECREATION
Enriching Our Quality of Life

Residents of all ages lead active lifestyles here. Whether one's leisure interests involve quiet moments in a place of solitude, sporting activities or interesting hobbies, Naperville is rich in opportunities. The Naperville Park District, the Forest Preserve District of DuPage County, Naper Settlement, the Naperville Area YMCA, the public schools, local organizations, area colleges, and private clubs all offer a choice of leisure activities.

THE NAPERVILLE PARK DISTRICT

When asked what makes Naperville's quality
of life so wonderful, most residents are quick to
credit the beautiful parks and outstanding
recreational programs offered by the Naperville
Park District, the second largest park district
in the state.

The park district owns or maintains more
than 2,300 acres of parkland throughout the
community, including the picturesque Riverwalk
in the heart of town. Neighborhood parks are
nestled among homes. Larger community parks
are scattered throughout Naperville, providing
athletic fields, ski trails, picnic shelters, skating
rinks, sled hills, tennis courts, and hiking trails for
all to enjoy.

The Naperville Park District also owns and
operates the community's beloved "swimming
hole," Centennial Beach. This former quarry was
purchased by thirty-three Naperville residents
during the Great Depression and donated to the
community for Naperville's 100th birthday.

With its zero-depth wading area, sandy beach, volleyball courts, picnic areas, large grassy hillside, and bath house, Centennial Beach is a popular hangout for teens and a favorite spot for parents and their children. A group of older adults, known as "The Beach Bums," reclaim a section of lawn almost every day throughout the summer, renewing old friendships and reliving their own years as youngsters at the Beach.

Golfers appreciate the Naperville Park District's two public golf courses, Springbrook and Naperbrook. These 18-hole courses are highly rated and are a favorite spot for serious golfers.

While the Naperville Park District is responsible for many outstanding programs, one of the finest is its New Horizons program. Designed for "anyone 55 or better," it offers everything from arts and crafts to international travel. The program is so much fun, some residents joke they can hardly wait until they turn 55!

One of Naperville's public golf courses.

The Naperville Park District offers many classes for children and adults.

THE RIVERWALK
Reflecting a Caring Community

Naperville's spectacular Riverwalk is the jewel in the crown of our community. Residents speak of it with enormous pride and visitors return to enjoy its peaceful flowing waters. Built by the community to celebrate its 150th birthday in 1981, the Riverwalk is a loving expression of Naperville's volunteer spirit. Townsfolk's donations of time, money and materials turned the once-blighted riverfront into a celebration of the city. The Riverwalk quickly became Naperville's pride and joy.

The park follows the meandering river throughout the heart of Naperville's downtown. Shepherd's crook light poles, antique-style benches, and distinctive brick pathways add an old-fashioned charm to this locale, linking the vibrant city with its historic past.

A gathering place for friends and families, the Riverwalk is also the setting for community activities throughout the year. Concerts, carnivals, art shows and more attract hundreds of families to the riverbanks. Children enjoy storytimes and magic shows during summer lunchtime performances, while braver souls listen to ghost stories "In the Park, In the Dark" as Halloween approaches. And, annually, artists display their works during a juried show.

THE FOREST PRESERVE DISTRICT OF DUPAGE COUNTY

The Riverwalk is also a link to other parks along the river. As part of a master plan, the Naperville Park District, the Forest Preserve District of DuPage County, and the City of Naperville are acquiring many of the remaining parcels of land along the West Branch of the DuPage River throughout Naperville. Their goal is to create a continuous greenway along the river, not only to preserve this local treasure, but to provide future recreational opportunities as well.

In addition, the Forest Preserve District owns or maintains numerous other parks, facilities, bike trails, and wilderness areas throughout the county, providing residents with more than 22,500 acres of open space and recreational opportunities.

6 2

THE NAPERVILLE AREA YMCA

Long before the Naperville Park District was established, and long before the Forest Preserve District was created, the YMCA was providing recreation for Naperville's families.

Inspired during a series of revival meetings in 1909, a group of local businessmen and ministers set out to establish a Young Men's Christian Association in Naperville. At first YMCA officials in Chicago told them that the town was too small for a Y, but the organizers persisted. With dinners served at a local church each evening before area men went out to seek contributions, and with pealing church bells signalling the end of each day's fund-raising efforts, the community campaign raised $22,260 in just 15 days. The cornerstone was laid in 1910, and a formal dedication of the building took place in March of 1911. For a while, it was known as "the largest Y in the smallest town" in the nation.

The Naperville Area YMCA has grown with Naperville's burgeoning population. It offers a wide variety of recreational opportunities for the community in numerous locations. The original building, known as the Kroehler Family Center, is located on Washington Street, and a second recreational facility, the 95th Street Family Center, opened in 1996 in the southern part of Naperville.

The Naperville Area YMCA Building constructed in 1910.

NAPER SETTLEMENT

For those who love history, Naper
Settlement offers a detailed glimpse into the lives
of those who made Naperville their home in the
1800s. Located on a hill overlooking the
paddleboat quarry and the Riverwalk, Naper
Settlement is the only nineteenth century living
history museum in the Chicagoland area. It tells
the story of how life changed as Naperville grew
from a frontier outpost in 1831 to a bustling turn-
of-the-century community in the opulent
Victorian era.

Costumed interpreters share almost-
forgotten skills and stories with visitors. History
comes alive as printers set type in their shop and
blacksmiths forge metal over red-hot coals.
Women provide for the needs of their families as
they quilt, spin wool, and cook over fires in the
hearth. Children practice penmanship in the one-
room schoolhouse and experience pioneer life in a
rustic log cabin. The rich Victorian-era traditions
of a successful local family capture everyone's
imagination at the Martin-Mitchell House, the
beautiful mansion built on the grounds in 1883.

Naper Settlement.

The thirteen-acre village offers walking tours and special events at various times throughout the year. Special events include "An Evening with the Lincolns," a Civil War encampment, trick-or-treating on the village grounds during the annual Halloween Happening, and "Christmas Memories" in the decorated village. Century Memorial Chapel is the setting for other events during the year and is also a favorite spot for local weddings.

The latest addition to the Settlement is the reconstructed Pre-Emption House, Naperville's first hotel and tavern built in 1834. The original building welcomed travelers on the road between Chicago and Galena and was the site of much of the town's activity. It again welcomes visitors as they enter Naper Settlement to experience the joys and hard work of days gone by.

The success of Naper Settlement is due to the tireless efforts of the Naperville Heritage Society, a dedicated staff and hundreds of volunteers. Founded in 1969 to save historical buildings and objects, the Heritage Society has relocated 18 endangered structures and reconstructed eight others.

ENTERTAINMENT
Adding a Splash of Fun!

Whatever one's interest, there is plenty to do in Naperville. For sports enthusiasts, the local high schools, clubs, and colleges have unending schedules of activity — including NCAA track and field championships where fans can volunteer or simply cheer from the stands. Many local families and businesses plan picnics a few miles away in Geneva, spending a fun-packed day watching the Kane County Cougars, a minor league professional baseball team. Others head for Chicago to watch the Bears, Bulls, Black Hawks, White Sox, or Cubs.

Those who prefer a night on the town can move to rhythm and blues at several popular spots. Many choose to sit around the coffee houses, meeting area musicians and listening to the guitar. Friends laugh as they recall old tunes while hanging around the piano bars at several downtown restaurants, while others lighten their spirits at the comedy clubs. Some just enjoy a good movie at one of the theater complexes in town.

Many Napervillians equate "entertainment" with "family," and this community reaches out to them. The Y sponsors "Family Friday Nights" so parents and kids can share quality time. Kids and teens can visit nearby museums, hands-on science exhibits, and an indoor amusement center. And many local organizations sponsor community-wide family festivals that are the highlight of the year. Ribfest, The Last Fling, and Oktoberfest — each of these festivals is also a major fund-raiser, and the money raised is invested back in the community to support important causes.

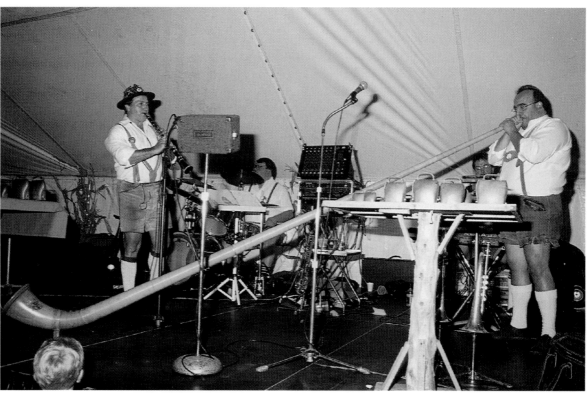

Oktoberfest, sponsored by the Naperville Rotary Club.

Frankie's Blue Room.

CULTURAL ACTIVITIES

Naperville offers a number of cultural opportunities for residents and visitors. The North Central College Performing Arts Association strives to celebrate fine arts within the community by offering a series of performances by nationally known artists.

Benedictine University broadens local horizons as well, with a Great Issues—Great Ideas lecture series that has brought internationally-respected speakers such as Dr. Jeane Kirkpatrick and Lady Margaret Thatcher to the area.

The Naperville Park District is an influential supporter of cultural events in the community and is a cosponsor of several efforts. For example, the Summer Place Theatre offers year-round performances, and the Magical Starlight Theatre presents children's entertainment.

The DuPage Symphony Orchestra, the Naperville Men's Glee Club, the Naperville Chorus, the Naperville Chamber Singers, and the Naperville Children's Chorus also help to give local talents a performing outlet and satisfy local appetites for good musical entertainment.

One of the best known and best loved musical groups is the Naperville Municipal Band. While its history extends well into the 1800s, today it continues its tradition of summer concerts in Central Park, a favorite ritual each Thursday evening.

Visual artists also find many opportunities to develop their talents in Naperville. The Naperville Art League, Gallery, and Fine Arts Center offers numerous classes, and the works of many members and guest artists are displayed in the gallery. A

Naperville Municipal Band.

most impressive display is the pre-juried Riverwalk Fine Art Fair, featuring artists from the United States and Canada. In addition, each July, the Naperville Woman's Club Annual Art Fair brings talented local and national artists to town, inviting them to display their works at the Martin-Mitchell House at Naper Settlement.

The Century Walk is another way local artists showcase their work. This innovative project is designed to weave various forms of public art into the fabric of Naperville's downtown. Each year, several artists are selected to create works that honor significant people, places, and events of twentieth century Naperville.

Naperville Men's Glee Club.

VOLUNTEER SPIRIT
Ripples of Caring and Kindness

People who live in Naperville recognize that this is a special town. There is a strong sense of community and cooperation here, made possible by a volunteer spirit that enhances every aspect of life.

Children collect food for the hungry and help their parents serve meals at a local shelter for the homeless. Youngsters in the Junior Exchange Club raise funds to fight child abuse. Teenage Police Explorers work the festivals, assisting with parking and security. And numerous student groups volunteer in the community, participating in "Pride in Our Parks," cleaning litter from the river in the annual "DuPage River Sweep," helping with literacy efforts, and doing many other worthwhile projects.

Parents and grandparents set the example of service to others, whether volunteering in the schools, at church, at Loaves and Fishes Food Pantry, or through one of the many volunteer organizations in town. Through its volunteer office, the City of Naperville is enriched by the talents of local residents. And school children benefit from the efforts of HURRAH — Happy, Upbeat, Recycled Retirees Actively Helping!

Local Girl Scouts help out the Jaycees Holiday Food Drive.

75

Naperville Police Volunteer Reading Program.

The community's most intense volunteer efforts are visible at each of Naperville's festivals — events that raise hundreds of thousands of dollars each year to help others.

Each Fourth of July holiday, the Naperville Park District and volunteers of the Exchange Club of Naperville cosponsor Ribfest, an award-winning event that features international rib vendors, musical entertainment, family activities and fireworks. This four-or five-day festival is billed as "Fun for the family . . . in support of the family," because all profits are returned to the community to fight child abuse and domestic violence. Since Ribfest began in 1988, the Exchange Club has given out over $1,000,000 to more than thirty local agencies and community programs that deal with the prevention of child abuse.

The Naperville Jaycees sponsor another award winner, The Last Fling, over Labor Day weekend. This summer send off brings a parade, carnival rides, food, and musical entertainment downtown for everyone's enjoyment. The money raised by the Jaycees has been donated to benefit hundreds of causes including the building of a wheelchair accessible playground on the Riverwalk, the Jaycee Marina on the paddleboat quarry, the new Naperville Area YMCA building, and Safety Town.

Each fall, the Rotary Club sponsors Oktoberfest, tempting families to enjoy tasty Bavarian food and polka to a lively German band. This successful fund-raiser has allowed the club to purchase an ambulance for a village in India, provide medical equipment for a hospital on St. Kitts in the Caribbean, and donate money for the construction of a plaza on the newest extension of the Riverwalk.

Through the efforts of the Junior Woman's Club, other volunteer organizations, and local businesses, $1,000,000 was raised to build a permanent Safety Town in Naperville. This small-scale community, used to teach young children about fire, traffic, and personal safety, is a national model and a tribute to a generous community.

Ribfest, sponsored by the Naperville Park District and Exchange Club of Naperville.

B U S I N

ESS

BUSINESS
Sustaining a Brimming Economy

Naperville is a booming community with demographics that attract new businesses and retain existing ones. Naperville enjoys low taxes, a low unemployment rate, a large skilled and highly-educated labor pool, and a thriving downtown retail/commercial sector. The city has a modern and well-maintained infrastructure. Easy access to major highways, Chicago's O'Hare and Midway airports, and Chicago's Union train station makes this a popular destination for businesses and their employees.

Several major companies are located in Naperville, including Amoco Research Center, Lucent Technologies, and Hewlett-Packard. Nalco Chemical Company and Allied Van Lines established their worldwide headquarters here. Together these businesses provide thousands of jobs and a valuable tax base.

The Naperville Visitors Bureau, founded in 1987 by the Naperville Area Chamber of Commerce, actively promotes the attractions, restaurants, and hotels in Naperville. The Visitors Bureau, made up of volunteers from the local business community, is an outstanding resource for tour operators and other visitors to town. The Naperville Development Partnership, comprised of city, chamber, park district, school districts, and local business representatives, monitors factors that impact the success and growth of local businesses. The partnership has compiled a database of information useful to any business considering expansion or a move to Naperville.

Metro West Building,
commonly known as the "N"
building due to its shape.

HISTORIC DOWNTOWN

Naperville's historic downtown is full of activity from morning until night. The brick sidewalks and shepherd's crook light poles highlight the old-fashioned charm of this district. Preserved and restored, 1800s-era buildings house a variety of charming shops, businesses and restaurants. Attractive benches offer shoppers and sightseers a place to rest while they enjoy the hometown flavor, beautiful flowers, and mature trees. The theme continues along the adjacent Riverwalk, further adding to the irresistible ambiance of downtown Naperville.

Naperville's success is due to dedication and planning. The Central Area Naperville Development Organization (CANDO) had the foresight and commitment to develop a plan that would tranform the downtown into a showpiece for the community.

The Downtown Merchants Association, a division of the Naperville Area Chamber of Commerce, was established to facilitate communication between the downtown merchants and to promote this quaint and popular downtown area. Shoppers look forward to annual sidewalk sales, craft fairs, and downtown holiday activities. "Grand Illumination" kicks off the holiday season in late November as Santa arrives and flips the switch, turning downtown into a winter wonderland of sparkling lights.

The vitality of Naperville's downtown section reflects the economic well-being of the area. Through volunteer efforts downtown will remain "the centerpiece of this community" for years to come.

SHOPPING

Whether looking for hidden treasures in a downtown jewelry store, vast selections in an expansive shopping center, or the convenience of a local retail store, the Naperville area offers shoppers a wide variety of choices.

Many residents enjoy spending time in historic downtown Naperville, browsing in bookstores, exploring antique shops, and stopping for ice cream on a hot summer's day. Several upscale national chains have opened here in recent years, drawing additional shoppers to this popular locale. Furniture, clothing, hardware, and gourmet foods can all be found in downtown Naperville, along with stores that serve everyday needs.

Numerous malls are located throughout the community as well, including the Fox Valley Center near Naperville in Aurora, Fifth Avenue Station a few blocks north of the historic downtown, and numerous neighborhood shopping areas. Together, they offer local residents and visitors a choice of upscale products, national labels, and discount merchandise.

DINING

Naperville has been called "an oasis of fine dining in the Western Suburbs" by Chicago's prestigious *North Shore Magazine*. That distinction is attributed to the selection of outstanding cuisine at a variety of prices to suit a myriad of lifestyles.

Fine French, Italian, Spanish, Japanese, American and other restaurants can all be found in Naperville. Seafood, hamburgers, barbecued ribs, steaks, salads and much more are served in elegant dining establishments, cozy cafes, relaxing outdoor eateries, family restaurants, fun micro-breweries, or exciting ethnic surroundings.

GOVER

M E N T

CITY SERVICES
Guiding the Current of Growth

The Municipal Center, gracefully situated along the banks of the DuPage River in downtown Naperville, overlooks the beautiful quarries and covered bridges of the community's famed Riverwalk. Many of the city's departments are located inside the building. Under the direction of a city manager, mayor, and eight-member city council, city employees provide quality services to area residents.

With Naperville identified as one of the fastest-growing cities in the country, providing such outstanding services is no easy task. It requires a great deal of planning, teamwork, and dedication. A special 1996 census determined that Naperville's population was over 110,000, and officials estimate that approximately 80 new residents move to Naperville every week.

To successfully deal with this growth, the city carefully created a Master Plan which maps out land use and services to ensure a balanced community. In 1992 the city tapped into Lake Michigan as a source of water and expanded the community's water-treatment capabilities. Operating the second-largest municipally-owned

electric distribution system in Illinois, Naperville maintains a significantly lower electric rate for customers than Commonwealth Edison. The city aggressively pursues road construction and repair, while forestry workers continue to plant hundreds of trees each year. In fact, Naperville has received the National Arbor Day Foundation's "Tree City USA" award for six consecutive years.

As the first Illinois community to offer curbside recycling, Naperville's efforts provide a model for the nation. Almost 90 percent of local residents participate in recycling efforts, one of the highest recycling rates in the country. Each year, more than 50 percent of the residential waste stream is diverted from our landfills.

The Finance Department has won several prestigious awards from the Government Finance Officers Association, the highest form of recognition in governmental financial reporting, accounting, and budgeting. And in 1995, the city's bond credit rating was upgraded from AA to AAA for the first time ever by both Moody's Rating Service and Standard and Poors. Naperville is the only Illinois community to have dual AAA ratings.

NAPERVILLE POLICE DEPARTMENT

The outstanding quality of life in Naperville is reflected in the community's safe neighborhoods, businesses, and city streets.

Of all Illinois cities with populations greater than 100,000, Naperville has the lowest violent crime rate, police budget, and per capita cost for police services. This is the result of a law-abiding citizenry and a professional police force that values expert training and cooperative relationships with the community.

The nationally accredited Naperville Police Department, located in a state-of-the-art facility on Aurora Avenue, employs top-notch personnel and trains them in the most advanced methods of crime prevention and investigation.

Adding to safety in the community is Naperville's enhanced 911 emergency communications system. When an emergency call is placed, the telephone number, address, and name of caller automatically appear on the police computer screen. This reduces the response time needed to provide emergency services.

The department also has embraced a policy of community-oriented policing and has created a true police/community partnership. In the Patrol Division, officers are assigned to permanent beats where they work closely with homeowners groups, businesses, and schools.

The Naperville Police Department has established a Neighborhood Family Resource Center that offers numerous positive prevention programs for families, as well as counseling and intervention. Children receive homework assistance and participate in a variety of activities, including Junior Achievement.

The Naperville Police Department conducts numerous educational programs in the schools, serving as role models and addressing important social issues. Additionally, there are many adult programs including the Community Radio Watch program. Trained volunteers regularly patrol Naperville's streets, greatly reducing crime in the community.

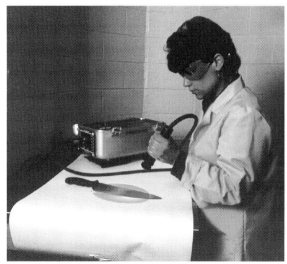

Evidence Room.

Community Watch.

NAPERVILLE FIRE DEPARTMENT

Like the police department, the nationally recognized Naperville Fire Department provides an exceptional level of protection for area residents. In addition to outstanding fire-fighting, emergency medical, investigations, inspections, and other basic services, the Naperville Fire Department offers several unique programs that place the city on the leading edge.

Naperville was the first community in the state to equip all of its fire engines with advanced life support medical equipment. By including cardiac monitor/defibrillators and other ambulance-type medical supplies on each of its engines, trained paramedics are able to efficiently respond to medical emergencies anywhere in the city. This enhanced system speeds the delivery of life-saving services to victims of auto accidents, trauma, cardiac arrest, and other medical emergencies.

The Technical Rescue Team, spearheaded by the Naperville Fire Department, includes firefighters from area fire departments. With advanced technical training and specialized equipment, the team successfully completes rescues under hazardous conditions, such as building collapses, excavation cave-ins, confined space emergencies, and elevated rescues. When a need for these services was identified, an appeal was made to local businesses, unions, and manufacturers. They responded generously and are part of this successful public/private partnership with donations of money and equipment.

Most residents have driven past the department's state-of-the-art Training Tower on Route 59 and some have witnessed flames or smoke rising from the facility. At this year-round

site, city and visiting professionals learn new techniques in fire-fighting, search and rescue, high-rise operations, and auto extrication.

Another unique service that many Naperville residents utilize is the Household Hazardous Waste program. In cooperation with the Illinois Environmental Protection Agency and the DuPage County Solid Waste Committee, the collection facility accepts nearly every type of hazardous product found in residents' homes.

TOWNSHIP GOVERNMENT

Naperville area residents also enjoy the services provided by local townships, a form of government that predates the United States Constitution. With boundaries that are approximately six miles square, five different townships exist at least partially within Naperville's borders. The largest is Lisle Township, followed in size by Naperville Township. Milton, DuPage, and Wheatland townships also provide special state-mandated services within the Naperville community.

Residential and commercial assessments, general assistance for the indigent, and road district funds are handled by the township offices. In addition, the townships offer special services for senior citizens and teens.

Naperville Township Building.

The spirit of volunteerism has long been the source of many new friendships, deep personal satisfaction, and a rich sense of community in Naperville. When the town was a small settlement on the banks of the DuPage River, voluntary donations of time, talent, money, and land started the community along an important path. This generosity encouraged the establishment of churches, a college, the library, the Naperville Area YMCA and Centennial Beach in the heart of town. As Naperville grew, similar efforts preserved the town's history, restored its business district, and created the beautiful Riverwalk. Today, a burgeoning population is drawing Naperville to southern fields, beyond the forks in the river where DuPage once traded with the Pottawatomis. Yet that generous volunteer spirit continues to reach out to our youth, our community, and those in need. As we move into the twenty-first century, it is this spirit that will allow Naperville to maintain its small-town atmosphere. It is this generous spirit that will also allow Naperville to meet new challenges as a community rich in caring and commerce.

N D U R E S

CORPORATE
IN EXCEL

PROFILES
NCE

NAPERVILLE AREA CHAMBER OF COMMERCE

Seize the future.
Grasp tomorrow's opportunity today.
Watch for it.
Recognize its potential.
Seize it.

There's a business revolution taking place.

It's a quiet channel of energy, driven by business, that is focused on directing broad-based economical and lifestyle changes — changes that will lead to greater self-reliance, community and stunning future opportunity.

It's a revolution to embrace change — one that will help businesses excel, prosper and flex with new environments.

It's a revolution that, for large and small businesses, compels the question, "Where are today's opportunities and how can I recognize them? How can my business grasp hold, take advantage and seize the future opportunity today?"

The Naperville Area Chamber of Commerce answers this competitive urgency with direction, action and specific goal-driven opportunities for business.

A Mission Statement of Purpose and Partnership

Within the Chamber's mission statement lie the words that embody the spirit of business: *Through the commitment and involvement of its members, the Naperville Area Chamber of Commerce provides business leadership for the benefit of the Naperville community by promoting economic opportunities, advocating the interests of business, providing members with education and resources and encouraging mutual support.*

The Naperville Chamber
Doing Business Better

The Naperville Area Chamber of Commerce is a diverse membership of businesses and business people who understand that to do business better, you must meet and exceed the competition. To exceed the competition in a complex marketplace, you must have collective competitive advantages. The Naperville Area Chamber of Commerce offers businesses distinct collective advantages through:

- Extensive information resources
- Comprehensive business exposure
- Community and interpersonal relationships
- Continuing education
- Specific marketing and advertising representation
- Proactive, visionary leadership
- Hands-on, on-the-spot, learning by doing
- Fun

Greeter programs allow access to new residents and business people.

These integrative marketing, business and personal development tools blend the best of business, community and professional individuals.

Competitive Advantages for All Businesses

The Naperville Area Chamber of Commerce is for everyone. We are not just for retailers, big business or small business. We are not a department of the City of Naperville. We are not stuffy and we are not political. We are your connection to success and competitive advantages.

Access

Members of the Chamber can access information and opportunities that are not available anywhere else. For example, exclusive mailing lists, educational programs, unique marketing opportunities and more are available only to our members.

Belonging

Chamber members belong to an important group of business people who are committed to their companies, work together to solve problems, share information and are committed to their community. Collectively we are a stronger voice for business.

Increasing Your Bottom Line

Money saving programs, direct discounts and services and more are offered only to Chamber members. In addition, members can take advantage of group buying opportunities and employee assistance programs.

Take Advantage

Members take advantage of a number of members-only programs and services. Consider that the Chamber receives hundreds of calls every week asking for information and referrals, and we only refer Chamber members.

Creating Awareness and Exposure

Your business has the opportunity to gain awareness and exposure to hundreds of other business people, residents or visitors. Every Chamber activity, event, publication or service is an opportunity for you to network — to make others aware of your business.

Your business deserves every chance for success. Do Business Better. Seize Opportunity Today. Join the Naperville Area Chamber of Commerce.

Naperville.net the Chamber's on-line business resource.

CITY OF NAPERVILLE

One of the fastest-growing cities in the country, Naperville is home to high-tech research and development centers, successful businesses, friendly neighborhoods, regionally-applauded festivals, cultural amenities, and historic attractions. With all of its advantages, including being only 30 miles from downtown Chicago, Naperville is the envy of DuPage County. Throughout the years, this dynamic community has handled population increases and economic expansion with insight and grace. Although the population has almost doubled each decade since 1950, the city has expanded and modernized its complex infrastructure while maintaining a small-town atmosphere and an outstanding quality of life.

Award-winning city government has played a key role in the acclaimed development of Naperville. Visionary planning has led to a vibrant downtown, inexpensive utilities, controlled growth, and public safety that ranks among the top in the nation. Strong intergovernmental cooperation and nationally-recognized financial management have allowed residents to receive an unusually high level of public service at minimal cost. The interaction of city departments with individual citizens and volunteer community groups has kept communications open and allowed residents to enjoy a deep sense of involvement and pride in their city.

Since 1969, Naperville has operated under the Council-Manager form of government. The city manager is the professional chief administrator for all city operations and is appointed by the city council. An eight-member city council and mayor are elected at large and hold regular public meetings at the Municipal Center, which houses most of the city's administrative offices. In the heart of Naperville, the Municipal Center overlooks the famed Riverwalk, a park built to celebrate the city's 150th anniversary, and one that attracts visitors year round.

Always on the leading edge in providing services to the community, the City of Naperville boasts dual AAA bond ratings, a nationally accredited and award-winning police department, state-of-the art fire and emergency medical protection, and numerous other exceptional services.

To provide up-to-date information about Naperville, the city has established a website at:

http://www.naperville.il.us

The site has over 300 pages of information and provides instantaneous access to anyone, anywhere in the world. Each day, the site receives over 1,300 hits, including inquiries from numerous cities in the United States and countries worldwide.

With council, mayor, city manager, and staff clearly focused on maintaining Naperville's exceptional quality of life, the city is the ideal place for families and businesses to relocate, assuring a bright future for this caring and dynamic community.

City of Naperville
400 S. Eagle Street
P.O. Box 3020
Naperville, Illinois 60566-7020
(630) 420-6111

THE NAPERVILLE DEVELOPMENT PARTNERSHIP

The Naperville Development Partnership is a unique cooperative effort that is designed to maintain and improve the economic vitality of Naperville. Joining together in this partnership are the City of Naperville, Naperville Area Chamber of Commerce, Naperville Park District, School Districts 203 and 204, Naperville and Lisle townships, and the business community at-large.

Incorporated as a not-for-profit corporation in 1994, the Naperville Development Partnership was established to strengthen our local economy by:

- Cultivating new business in Naperville
- Helping existing businesses expand
- Encouraging existing businesses to remain in Naperville
- Facilitating and promoting new business development programs
- Cultivating and maintaining a strong labor pool
- Maintaining a strong and diverse economy to further enhance the community's quality of life

To promote Naperville's economic vitality, the partnership is focusing its efforts on three main areas: marketing, retention, and information.

Marketing

To ensure the city's current and future competitive position, Naperville is promoting its numerous advantages and competitive edge — good schools, fine jobs, exceptional quality of life, and low crime rate — through a proactive, sustained marketing strategy directed at targeted businesses and industries.

Retention

To retain our healthy business base, the Naperville Development Partnership assists existing businesses by:

- Serving as a liaison to municipal agencies
- Facilitating resources for assistance with expansion, capital improvements, and comprehensive planning
- Calling on businesses personally to identify problems, find solutions, learn about key business issues and trends, and determine why businesses stay and expand in Naperville

Information

As prospective businesses evaluate Naperville as a possible location for their facilities, obtaining accurate information about the community is essential. To meet the demand for such information, the Naperville Development Partnership is developing a comprehensive strategic database of information, including:

- Federal, state, city, community, and financial resources
- Current infrastructure
- Community leaders, development partners, and networking opportunities
- Available land parcels and office/retail/warehouse space
- Local and regional demographics
- Municipal and community policies, procedures, fees, and regulations

The Naperville Development Partnership is helping the community position itself for well-planned, well-managed business growth while maintaining the qualities that have made Naperville a "destination city" for residents and businesses alike.

Working together, members of this public and private development partnership will ensure a dynamic, exciting future for both the residential and business communities of Naperville.

Naperville Development Partnership
131 W. Jefferson Avenue
Naperville, Illinois 60540
(630) 355-4141
(800) 642-7829

BUSINESS, FIN
PROFESSIONS

ANCE, AND

The Amoco Research Center is located along Interstate 88 in Naperville.

THE AMOCO RESEARCH CENTER IN NAPERVILLE

Amoco Corporation is one of the largest publicly traded producers of crude oil, natural gas and petrochemicals, and is ranked the 13th largest industrial corporation in the United States. Amoco was founded in 1889 in Whiting, Indiana. Throughout its 100 year history, the company's success has been closely tied to technology and community involvement. Today, Amoco's 43,000 employees in 40 countries are dedicated to continuous progress in improving the quality of products and services, a respect for the environment, and a determination to ensure that operations do not adversely affect the air, water and land of the communities where we operate.

Amoco has a long history in Naperville that began with service stations and has evolved to include the Amoco Research Center on Warrenville Road and the new Split Second University training center for convenience store operators.

Amoco in Naperville

Since 1970, Amoco's petroleum products and chemicals sectors have conducted exploratory and technical research at the 178-acre Amoco Research Center in Naperville located in the Research and Development Corridor along Interstate 88. Today, about 1,000 skilled professionals at the center produce the scientific and technical innovations that help Amoco continually improve its products and services.

Hundreds of products we use every day are the result of technological breakthroughs at the center. For example, Amoco scientists developed the raw material for polyester. The material is used in fabrics, carpeting, cassette tapes, compact disc cases, microfilm and plastic containers — including the first plastic soft drink bottles. Amoco Ultimate Gasoline was also formulated here, and today is the gasoline ranked number one by consumers.

Putting Safety First

Employees at the research center are committed to working safely and being prepared to respond during an emergency. Employees receive rigorous training and use state of the art equipment to ensure a safe workplace. Each summer, the center's emergency response team and the Naperville Fire Department conduct a drill to ensure all the necessary people, equipment and supplies are ready on a moments notice should a real-life incident occur.

Supporting our Neighbors

Amoco has a long-standing commitment to support our neighbors by backing the social and cultural institutions in the communities where our employees live and work. Approximately 1,800 Amoco employees live in Naperville. Through volunteerism, local Amoco employees dedicate thousands of hours to local nonprofits and schools each year. After retirement, many people remain actively

Hundreds of products we use every day are the result of technological breakthroughs by Amoco's researchers in Naperville, including polyester fabrics and containers.

involved in their communities through a volunteer group called AmoCares. On average, AmoCares members dedicate over 10,000 hours of service to local charities. In addition to volunteer efforts, Amoco Foundation provides grants to support local nonprofits and schools offering programs designed to make math, science and technology interesting and fun for area youth. Grants totaling roughly $100,000 are presented to local nonprofits and schools each year. In 1996, Amoco Foundation also provided an emergency response grant of $25,000 to the American Red Cross to provide food, clothing and shelter to Naperville residents affected by severe flooding.

Protecting our Environment

Amoco has been recognized by the Conservation Foundation of DuPage County for its long-standing commitment to protect the environment. Programs at the research center range from high-tech energy conservation efforts to working with conservationists to clean the DuPage River and restore endangered species. The center's resource recovery plant generates nearly all of the energy required to operate the site through a natural-gas-fired cogeneration system. The scientists at the center are also involved in ongoing research efforts to develop cleaner burning transportation fuels, to enhance process technology and to improve methods for waste disposal and minimization. Working with conservationists from the Wisconsin Department of Natural Resources, the center participates in the Trumpeter Swan Breeding Program. The goal of the program is to help restore the habitat and to support repopulation of the nearly extinct trumpeter swan. Since the program's inception in 1992, each spring cygnets have been hatched and raised by a pair of adult swans residing on Amoco's 11-acre lake.

Building upon the historic ties between Amoco and the people of DuPage County, the future for both looks promising.

Amoco is working with the Wisconsin Department of Natural Resources Trumpeter Swan Breeding Program to restore the habitat and population of the nearly extinct animals.

AMERITECH

Ameritech, one of the world's largest communications companies, helps more than thirteen million customers keep in touch. Ameritech provides customers what they want — one-stop communications, the convenience of a single bill, attentive customer service, and a century of reliability. The company meets a broad range of customers' needs with local and long distance, cellular, paging, cable TV, security monitoring, automated library services, Internet access, and on-line services.

The company also exports its communications skills and financial resources to national and international markets. As a result, Ameritech's growing businesses today reach customers in fifty states and forty countries. Ameritech is creating dozens of new information, entertainment, and interactive services for homes, businesses, and governments around the world.

The most important new growth opportunity for Ameritech is long distance. The company stands ready, pending government approval, to move into the marketplace with a state-of-the-art long distance network and an easy-to-understand, competitive package of innovative long distance products for all customer segments. Ameritech already provides long distance service to more than one million cellular phone customers and in several foreign countries.

An important economic force in Illinois, Ameritech has over 23,000 employees in the state. The Ameritech network in Illinois is one of the most advanced in the United States.

Ameritech offers Naperville residents a new choice in cable TV. Called *americast*™, it gives Naperville residents more programming options via its expanded selection of eighty to ninety channels and imaginative programming developed through a partnership which includes The Walt Disney Company. Ameritech's Naperville-based Video Operations Center and Regional Design Center employ approximately 100 people.

A Naperville Area Chamber of Commerce member since 1965, Ameritech has supported the community in a variety of ways. The company has given financial grants to Little Friends and North Central College, and was the primary sponsor of the 1996 Ameritech Sing-along produced by Naperville Community Television (NCTV). Ameritech also supports the community through robust employee volunteerism by its nearly 400 employees in the area, as well as corporate and employee support of the Crusade of Mercy.

W. BRAND BOBOSKY

Few exemplify Naperville's community spirit better than attorney Brand Bobosky — a true professional who is dedicated to serving his clients, his community, and his family.

Symbolizing the central role that he plays in our town, Bobosky's law office is conveniently located at the corner of Chicago Avenue and Main Street. While offering a wide variety of legal services, he concentrates in commercial and residential real estate transactions, business and commercial law, estate planning and wills, and personal injury law.

Bobosky's educational and legal credentials are extensive. A lifelong resident of DuPage County, he received undergraduate degrees from Benedictine University and the University of Notre Dame du Lac and a Juris Doctor degree from the University of Illinois. He has directed sophisticated legal activities for several major public companies and performed personalized legal services for many residents and local businesses who appreciate the fact that he is knowledgeable, affordable, and friendly.

Nicknamed "Naperville's Idea Man," Brand Bobosky's community involvement is well recognized. In the 1970s, he and his wife conceptualized the extremely successful Little Friends, Inc. Auction which annually raises nearly $100,000 to support a variety of programs for individuals with disabilities.

Bobosky suggested in 1989 that CANDO sponsor annual holiday lighting on buildings so that, each winter, the downtown now glistens with little white lights that complement the similarly illuminated trees. He was also instrumental in the Rotary Club of Naperville bringing its annual Oktoberfest to the community.

Most recently, he introduced and promoted Century Walk, the creation of public art throughout Naperville's greater downtown, permanently portraying Naperville's significant twentieth century people, places, and events.

Throughout the years, Bobosky has been involved in many local business organizations and other service clubs, as well. He has served as president of the Naperville Area Chamber of Commerce, the Naperville Jaycees, and Little Friends, Inc.

Supporting his efforts throughout the community is Brand's wife, Mary Ann, director of community relations for Naperville Community Unit School District 203. Together, they have four children, three grandchildren, and many friends who recognize the worthwhile contributions they both have made to our city as professionals and as citizens.

W. Brand Bobosky
Lawyer
50 W. Chicago Avenue, Naperville 60540
(630) 355-5555

CRESTVIEW BUILDERS

Crestview Builders, one of the area's top home-building and land-development firms, has been an integral part of Naperville's dynamic growth since co-owners Ronald Wehrli and Michael Steck founded the company in 1978.

Since its inception, Crestview Builders has developed seventeen subdivisions and built more than 1,500 custom homes in Naperville and nearby communities. Known for quality work, spacious floor plans, attractive developments, and good value, the company works with transferees, first-time home buyers, and many satisfied second- and third-time buyers who are "moving up" as their families and incomes grow.

Crestview Builders has been one of the area's finest custom home builders for several years, designing and building 80 to 100 homes annually. In 1996, *Professional Builder Magazine* included Crestview Builders in its Giant 400 list, which ranks the top home builders in the country.

Among the Naperville subdivisions developed by Crestview Builders is Olesen Estates, originally the District 203 Wohead Farm school site. When completed, the subdivision will be home to 120 families. Crestview Builders is also developing Prairie Crossing, a 150-lot subdivision at 103rd Street near Book Road. The company also developed Hobson Meadows, Fox Meadows, Norwood Court, Crestview Knolls, Countryside, and Heritage Creek.

Sixth-generation Napervillians, Wehrli and Steck are descendents of families that settled the Naperville area in the 1880s. The men credit their knowledge of the area and good working relationships with subcontractors for their success. "We were in the right place at the right time," admits Wehrli, the firm's president. "We recognized that growth was going to happen, and we wanted to make sure that development

occurred in a way that was in keeping with the Midwestern, down-home traditions that are such an important part of Naperville. We treat people fairly — the way we like to be treated — and our clients appreciate it."

Crestview Builders has participated in the Cavalcade of Homes on numerous occasions and is the winner of many coveted awards. It is a member of the Northern Illinois Home Builders Association and the Naperville Area Chamber of Commerce.

"We invite visitors to walk through our model homes and view some of the floor plans we have available," adds Wehrli. "We'll gladly arrange to sit down and show interested visitors how our architect can modify those designs and create a beautiful custom home for them."

Crestview Builders, Inc.
1416 Dunrobin Road
Naperville, Illinois 60540
(630) 961-1144

FIRST CHICAGO

First Chicago has been an important part of the Naperville community for a number of years, originally as Gary-Wheaton Bank. The merger of First Chicago Corporation and NBD Bancorp marked the joining of two leading financial institutions that, together, provide a tradition of nearly 200 years of banking expertise to the community.

With main offices located at the corner of Hobson Road and Naper Boulevard and branches in local Dominick's Finer Food stores, First Chicago provides customers with an unparalleled range of products and services. The largest bank in the state, First Chicago has over 130 branches and 700 ATMs, providing customers the luxury of being able to bank at their "hometown" bank, wherever they are.

First Chicago customers choose from a full range of deposit accounts, including checking, savings, money mar-

ket, and certificates of deposit. The loan menu includes personal and auto loans, home-equity loans, home mortgages, equity lines of credit, and small business loans. As a leader in electronic banking, First Chicago offers on-line bill payment, as well as home banking through several popular computer software programs.

A neighborhood bank, First Chicago is dedicated to the community it serves so well. Officers have been active on boards of Little Friends, the School District 203 Business Education Partnership, United Way, and the Naperville Area Chamber of Commerce. Employees volunteer their time at Ribfest and the Last Fling and race in Naperville's Grand Prix. The bank has been a strong financial supporter of the Edward Health and Fitness Center 10-K Run, Little Friends, the School District 204 student recognition banquet, the construction of Safety Town and the Pre-Emption House, the

Naperville Area YMCA capital campaign, and numerous other community initiatives.

Most heartwarming is the involvement of First Chicago's employees with students at Scott Elementary School. In a partnership with School District 203, First Chicago runs a bank at the school. Fourth and fifth graders are actual tellers and personal bankers, accepting deposits, counting cash, writing receipts, verifying funds, and balancing statements. They help other students correctly fill out deposit slips, record deposits in their ledgers, and calculate their balances. It is a valuable partnership that reflects the bank's commitment to this community and its children.

First Chicago
The First National Bank of Chicago
1212 Hobson Road
Naperville, Illinois 60540
(630) 961-1011

HARRIS BANK NAPERVILLE

On March 15, 1957, Harris Bank Naperville opened its doors, paying 2% interest on savings accounts, and 3% on Certificates of Deposits. The first sentence of its "Statement of Policy" read "The Bank is in business to serve the financial needs of the residents of Naperville and vicinity." The Bank, known then as the Bank of Naperville, has maintained this goal as its guiding principle through four presidents and 40 years, while growing to more than $526,000,000 in assets.

Unlike most banks of the time — and today — the Bank of Naperville was founded by a large group of local stockholders, who elected Herbert Rumsfeld the first Chairman of the Board, and John Corkill the first President.

Part of the goal of this local group of founders was to insure the Bank would be responsive to the local community. This is still a paramount concern today according to Frank Slocumb, President. "Our involvement in the Naperville community has been the foundation of the bank's purpose and success — both in our early development and today," Slocumb said.

The new bank building, located on Washington Street at Fifth Avenue, brought the first drive-up window service to Naperville, staying open until 4:30 p.m., two hours longer than the lobby. Another unusual feature at the Bank changed the common practice of the time of charging to make deposits to their accounts.

Today the Bank operates 15 drive-up lanes at five offices, some staffed seven days a week from as early as 7:00 a.m. to as late as 8:00 p.m. In addition to the original bank site at Washington Street and Fifth Avenue, the Bank today serves its customers from branches at Washington Street at Aurora Avenue, Hawthorne Square, Brighton Commons, Diehl Road, as well as through Cash Stations® all over Chicagoland. The original building has grown in size from three floors of 2,800 square feet to more than 40,000 square feet and the bank employees to more than 200 individuals.

In 1983 the Bank again took a significant step "to serve the financial needs of the residents of Naperville and vicinity" when shareholders approved an offer to join Harris Bankcorp, the parent holding company for Harris Trust and Savings Bank in Chicago. Today, the Harris organization combined with the resources of the Bank of Montreal, spans North America from Canada to the U.S. and Mexico, with more than 140 locations in the Chicagoland area alone.

Harris Bank Naperville is proud to celebrate 40 years of service to the community, and looks forward to helping local individuals and businesses explore the financial opportunities of the future.

Harris Bank Naperville
503 N. Washington
Naperville, Illinois 60563
(630) 420-3500

MIDAMERICA FEDERAL

One Customer At A Time for 75 Years.

Naperville, IL — For 75 years, MidAmerica Federal Savings Bank has endeavored to fulfill the financial needs of its customers one customer at a time. This straightforward customer service philosophy clearly speaks to the venerable institution's long-time success as a community bank.

After successfully servicing the Cicero/Berwyn community for over 50 years, MidAmerica Federal established its first Naperville branch in 1974. The ultra-modern facility opened a new and exciting chapter for the bank. Consider that in 1974 Naperville was a mid-sized, far-west suburb with a population of just 28,000. Who could imagine that 23 years later with four bustling Naperville branches, MidAmerica Federal would be acknowledged as one of the leading home mortgage lenders and financial institutions in this burgeoning suburb known nationwide as a technological center of creativity.

In addition to four full-service Naperville branches, MidAmerica Federal's commitment to innovation and to the community led to the opening of the first fully operational in-school bank in the Midwest in 1995. The Green and Gold Bank opened at Waubonsie Valley High School and today successfully operates as a MidAmerica Federal facility for students and teachers during school hours.

MidAmerica Federal has built a leading position in the financial services industry by offering customers a wide variety of financial products and services to meet the needs of a diversified marketplace. Fundamental to meeting these varied financial needs is the ability to provide innovative, current products and services that include traditional savings products, alternative investment services, fixed and adjustable rate home mortgage loans, home equity loans, consumer loans, Totally FREE Checking, Bank-By-Phone, VISA Check Card, and a network of Automatic Teller Machines. Product innovation combined with a dedication to exceptional customer service allow the Bank to continue its leadership position.

Operating from a Chicagoland network of 21 offices, including Northwestern Savings Division branches, MidAmerica Federal also strives to help build stronger communities in each of the locations it serves. The cornerstone of MidAmerica Federal's customer service philosophy rests on the ability to make a positive difference in the lives of those who live in the communities we serve. For example it is common to find MidAmerica Federal officers and employees actively involved in service organizations throughout Naperville from the United Way to the YMCA, Rotary, Naperville Exchange Club, Naperville Community School Foundation and many more. This active participation benefits the community and allows MidAmerica Federal to better understand and develop products that specifically meet the needs of Naperville families.

MidAmerica remains committed to making a special effort in the Naperville community and to responding to our unique customers, one at a time. This sharp focus guides the bank on its continuing journey to build and nurture a long-term relationship with the Naperville community and the families with whom we work and live.

MidAmerica Federal Savings Bank
1001 S. Washington Street • (630) 420-1001
9 E. Ogden Avenue • (630) 420-8000
3135 Book Road • (630) 305-6100
1308 S. Naper Boulevard • (630) 420-8400

PEOPLE YOU CAN COUNT ON® IN ILLINOIS

A guiding principle that is central to Pro Staff's operating philosophy has helped build its reputation for providing "people you can count on." That principle is that clients will receive better service and better results from a company that cares about and is committed to the selection and development of its independent workers. Accordingly, Pro Staff takes steps to ensure that its people are right for each job and are given the tools to succeed, including: thorough interviewing and testing; ongoing training and education; dedicated support from staffing specialists; values assessment and matching between clients and employees; and client and job orientation.

One of the country's foremost temporary and flexible staffing service companies, Pro Staff operates offices nationwide with a strong market presence in the Greater Chicagoland area. An acknowledged industry leader in attracting and retaining outstanding personnel, Pro Staff meets client staffing needs ranging from short-term positions to outsourcing of entire departments and programs. Its mission is to partner with customers to manage their overall human resources efficiently and cost-effectively, and to consistently deliver strategies and services that far exceed customer expectations. Founded in Minneapolis in 1982 with just three offices, Pro Staff's rapid expansion is underpinned by strong local performance. "Our Naperville office is one of the reasons we have been able to grow so quickly in the Chicago market," comments Chicago General Manager Steve Wolfe.

Pro Staff assures total client satisfaction through such measures as productivity assessments, performance-based pricing and, where appropriate, on-site management of Pro Staff workers. Because of the care it takes in finding, training, managing and retaining people, Pro Staff can guarantee total satisfaction: if clients are dissatisfied, they pay nothing at all.

In addition to staffing administrative, clerical, technical, and light industrial positions, Pro Staff offers specialized support in accounting, information technology, creative services, and customer service through its specialty staffing divisions. Chicago-area locations include Downtown Chicago, Downers Grove, O'Hare, Rolling Meadows, Lincolnshire, Mc Henry, the IT Consulting Professionals office and the Accounting Professionals office.

To contact the Pro Staff office nearest you, call 1 (800) 938-WORK.

Pro Staff
1567 N. Aurora Road
Suite 135
Naperville, Illinois
(630) 428-8300

STANDARD FEDERAL BANK

"The success of Standard Federal Bank is anchored by our dedication to providing customers with highly competitive financial products as well as outstanding service, and a vow to remain a community organization genuinely concerned about the people and areas we serve," explains David Mackiewich, president of the locally based institution. To experience the bank's commitment to excellence, Mackiewich invites you to visit Standard's Naperville office, located at 425 W. Ogden Avenue, across from Naperville North High School.

Founded in 1909 in Chicago, Standard Federal has since developed a strong branch network that now serves the city and suburbs. Despite many changes through the years, two important things have remained constant: Standard's resolve to ensure the highest level of professional assistance and it's responsiveness in providing the financial tools you need.

Savers, for instance, will find our innovative CDs offer some of the best rates and most desirable terms in the area. In addition, a variety of other deposit products are available, such as savings accounts, money market accounts, Christmas club accounts, plus checking accounts and more.

New and used car buyers will save money with affordable auto loans that feature some of the lowest rates available. Or, for those seeking an inexpensive way to pay for home improvements or a child's college tuition, Standard offers attractively priced home equity loans and lines of credit. And if you're looking for a better deal on revolving credit, inquire about our competitive MasterCard and Visa credit cards.

Home buyers can make their dreams come true with a variety of mortgage alternatives. Whether it's an adjustable or fixed-rate mortgage, an extremely low down payment or no up-front fees, Standard has the right plan

for every situation — all with a guaranteed great rate! Home mortgages are provided through Standard Financial Mortgage Corporation, a wholly owned subsidiary of the bank.

For those interested in dependable insurance coverage or alternative investments, we can help with our other subsidiaries, SFB Insurance Agency and SFB Investments, Inc. Both offer the top notch professional assistance with annuities, life insurance, long-term care coverage, discount stock brokerage and more.

For details about these and other exciting financial products and services, simply call Standard's Naperville office at **(630) 357-4949**. We'll be happy to help you in any way we can!

Standard Federal Bank for savings
425 West Ogden Avenue
Naperville, Illinois 60563
(630) 357-4949

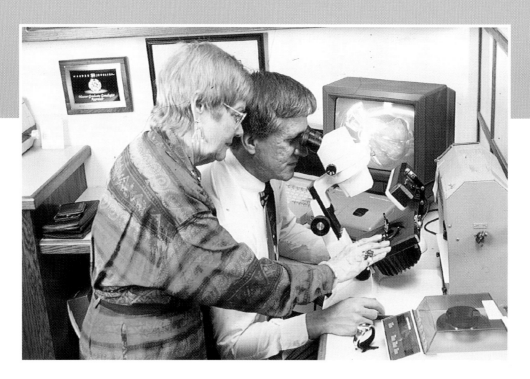

TOENNIGES JEWELERS

Toenniges Jewelers is, literally, one of the gems of Naperville's historic downtown. A charming shop, its windows, shelves, and counters are brimming with precious stones, handcrafted jewelry, quality watches, and unusual collectibles.

Dorcas Pearcy has served three generations of customers since she and her late husband, Dr. Frederick Toenniges, purchased the store in 1948. She credits the store's success to its friendly ambiance and personalized service.

Toenniges' success is also due to the high level of professional skills its employees have achieved. Manager Michael Harrington is one of just ten jewelers in the United States to earn a Master Graduate Gemologist Appraiser designation. The jewelry store is a member of the American Gem Society.

Designing jewelry is another unusual facet of Toenniges Jewelers.

Using gold, silver, and gems, the shop's artisans create beautiful, one-of-a-kind pieces. Toenniges recently won a design competition sponsored by the Illinois Jewelers Association. They even designed 14K gold and sterling silver charms, replicas of Century Memorial Chapel.

Toenniges Jewelers is a popular place to purchase a new watch or have an older timepiece repaired. In fact, it is watchmaking that gave this business its start many years ago. In the 1940s, Frederick Toenniges was a music professor at North Central and Illinois Benedictine Colleges and director of the Aurora Symphony Orchestra. Dorcas, with a music degree from North Central, sang with the Chicago Symphony Chorus. Since Frederick Toenniges had a passion for watch repair too, the couple purchased McEwan Jewelers, which they renamed the Tic-Toc Shop and later changed the name to Toenniges Jewelers.

Their favorite expression, still used today, was, "We can repair anything but the crack of dawn or a broken heart."

An important part of Naperville's business community, Toenniges Jewelers has been deeply involved in the Naperville Area Chamber of Commerce, CANDO, and the Downtown Merchants Association. It has also generously responded to numerous community fund-raisers.

"In our business, we don't sell food, clothing, or shelter," says Pearcy. "But we do sell the things that allow people to express their love and affection for others." Through its contributions to the community, Toenniges Jewelers often expresses that same affection for Naperville.

Toenniges Jewelers
33 West Jefferson
Naperville, Illinois
(630) 355-1321

WEGNER PLUMBING COMPANY

Wegner Plumbing, founded by Russ Wegner in 1975, opened its first Naperville store in 1987. Over the years, it has grown, added a beautiful Kohler registered showroom, and moved to its current location at 701 Frontenac Road in northwest Naperville, north of Fox Valley Mall.

Primarily a residential plumbing business, Wegner Plumbing provides new construction installation for custom home builders, as well as remodelling installations and service work at existing homes and businesses. The firm's service/maintenance system ensures same-day plumbing service to customers in need.

Wegner Plumbing added the Kohler registered showroom several years ago, allowing customers to see the plumbing products and colors first hand. The 1800-square-foot area displays the latest in upscale products, including

Kohler whirlpool tubs, body spas, kitchen sinks, pedestal sinks, toilets, and faucetries. Every color that Kohler makes is displayed somewhere in the showroom. In addition to Kohler, Wegner Plumbing showcases Jacuzzi tubs, Oasis tubs, Moen faucets, and top-of-the-line Grohe faucets from West Germany. The fully trained staff is always on hand to provide knowledgeable, personal service.

"We work with our customers professionally and honestly," says owner Russ Wegner. "Integrity is an important part of our business."

Russ Wegner also believes that his company should give back to the community that has provided him with so many opportunities. The firm sponsors local girls' and boys' baseball teams through the Naperville Baseball Association. Wegner Plumbing also supports high school events, college

activities, Ribfest, and The Last Fling through sponsorships or advertising.

Wegner Plumbing is a member of the Naperville Area Chamber of Commerce, the Plumbing and Mechanical Contractors Association of Northern Illinois, the Illinois and National Associations of Plumbing, Heating and Cooling Contractors, the Quality Service Contractors Association, and the Northern Illinois Home Builders Association. "We have pride in our company, community, and profession," Wegner adds. "We offer services that many of our competitors do not, because we want our clients to become satisfied, lifetime customers."

Wegner Plumbing
701 Frontenac Road
Naperville, Illinois 60563
(630) 369-0151

HEALTH CARE

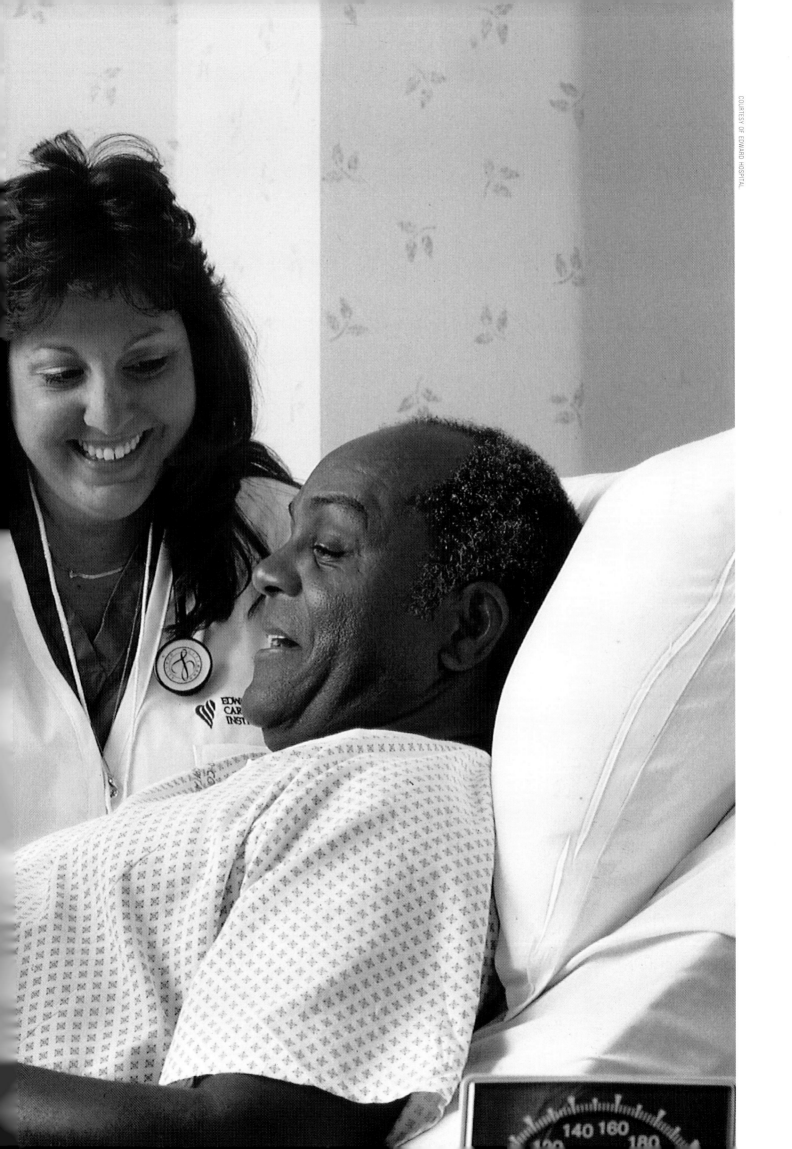

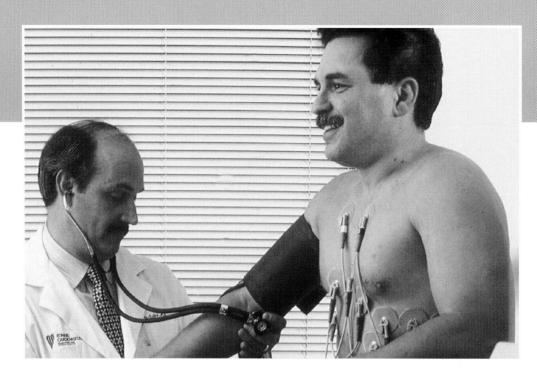

EDWARD HEALTH SERVICES CORPORATION

Helping Naperville stay well

Edward Health Services Corporation (EHSC) is committed to helping you and your family stay well. As Naperville's comprehensive healthcare provider, we offer everything from experienced primary care to prevention-minded wellness screenings to highly specialized medical services. EHSC facilities are located throughout the communities we share to make staying well top-of-mind and convenient.

Edward Hospital is a 169-bed, state-of-the-art facility located at 801 South Washington Street in Naperville. Throughout our history, Edward Hospital has introduced a number of healthcare innovations such as all private hospital rooms and medically-based fitness.

Much of our innovation can be attributed to our staff. Our physicians, nurses, therapists, and technicians are experienced, motivated professionals focused on providing the very best patient care. Working together, our staff is able to provide a wide range of medical, surgical, OB/GYN, pediatric, and rehab services, as well as Level II trauma capabilities.

Edward Hospital is the cornerstone of EHSC's Naperville campus which is also home to the Edward Health & Fitness Center, Edward Cardiovascular Institute, Edward Cancer Center, Edward Medical Office Buildings I and II, and Linden Oaks Hospital.

For general Edward Hospital information, call (630) 961-4949.

Primary Care

Family First represents Edward Hospital's commitment to families. We put families first because we believe the family experience is a vital part of a happy, healthy life.

Family First includes a variety of programs. Our pediatricians, obstetricians, neonatologists, and family practice physicians provide expert care and support.

Parents are encouraged to visit our birthing suites — private rooms conducive to family-centered birthing. Each room is outfitted with the latest monitoring technology, as well as comforting amenities. Parents also appreciate our Neonatal Intensive Care Nursery, where ill and premature infants receive advanced neonatal care.

If you'd like to learn more about Family First, sign up for a class, or schedule a birthing suite tour, call (630) 961-4941.

The **Edward Healthcare Centers** (EHC) bring expert primary care services into the communities we share. At these Centers — located in Naperville and Bolingbrook — individuals can seek everything from an annual physical to immunizations to mammography.

The Edward Healthcare Center/Bolingbrook is staffed by experienced primary care physicians, nurses, and support staff who provide *immediate care* — the kind designed to treat non-life-threatening medical conditions. This team can take care of everything from

broken bones to high fevers to X-rays.

To make accessing quality healthcare as convenient as possible, each EHC location offers expanded hours.

The EHC in Bolingbrook is located at 130 North Naperville Road. Its hours are: 7 a.m. to 10 p.m., Monday through Friday, 8 a.m. to 6 p.m., Saturday, Sunday, and holidays. Immediate care is also available at these times. Call (630) 378-3400 to learn more.

The EHC in Naperville is located at 95th Street and Book Road. Call (630) 355-2667 for more information.

The **Edward Women's Center for Health** (WCH) was founded on the belief that the best healthcare results from patient and physician working together. Our progressive approach focuses on wellness: *preventing illness* through education and empowerment.

The WCH staff includes physicians, a nurse practitioner, a certified nurse midwife, counselors, a registered dietitian, and a massage therapist, all of whom provide healthcare that addresses both body and mind. Our primary care physician diagnoses and

treats a range of medical conditions, and our obstetricians/gynecologists provide complete pregnancy, childbirth, and postpartum care.

To learn more about the Edward Women's Center for Health, call (630) 416-3300.

Specialized Medical Services

The **Edward Cardiovascular Institute** (ECI) was created to actively support the cardiovascular health of our community. The ECI's expert medical team includes cardiologists, surgeons, and clinical nurse specialists. Many of these professionals have trained at some of the nation's premier cardiology centers, including the Mayo Clinic.

In addition, a number of ECI physicians are involved in clinical research investigating new treatments and medications. This research orientation allows us to offer our patients the most advanced thinking in the field today.

The Edward Cardiovascular Institute is located at 120 Spalding Drive on the Edward Hospital campus. For more information, call (630) 527-2802.

More than 12 million Americans are living with cancer as they go to school, work, or enjoy time with family and friends. Increasingly, *living* with cancer is a reality, as medical advances make treatments more effective and side effects less disruptive.

The **Edward Cancer Center** is committed to supporting people experiencing cancer. Patients can access outpatient treatment, rehabilitation, and support services, in addition to complete preventive education and screenings.

Cancer Center oncologists have trained at some of the nation's most prestigious university medical centers. These physicians regularly participate in clinical trials that evaluate the very latest treatments. They're also able to access advanced therapies — including bone marrow transplants — through our affiliation with the Cardinal Bernardin Cancer Center.

To learn more about the Edward Cancer Center, Call (630) 527-3788.

Every moment is critical during a medical emergency. The staff at the Edward Hospital **Emergency Department** is prepared to expertly handle everything from acute trauma to broken bones. Our Level II trauma facilities and special pediatric emergency equipment help us provide advanced, thorough care.

To ensure that patients with minor emergencies receive the care they need as quickly as possible, we created the **ER Fast Track**. Patients with injuries such as a simple fracture or laceration are treated right in the ER Fast Track, which is staffed by an experienced team of emergency medical professionals. ER Fast Track patients are usually treated and released within one hour of arrival.

For optimal patient convenience, *immediate care* is available at the Edward Healthcare Center in Bolingbrook.

The ER Fast Track is located adjacent to the Edward Hospital Emergency Department. Its hours are: 5 p.m. to 10 p.m., weekdays, 1 p.m. to 10 p.m., weekends and holidays. The Emergency Department is open 24 hours a day, seven days a week. Immediate Care is open 7 a.m. to 10 p.m., weekdays, 8 a.m. to 6 p.m., weekends and holidays.

Linden Oaks is a private psychiatric hospital located on the Edward Hospital campus. The staff of psychiatrists, psychologists, and social workers is trained in a variety of disciplines, providing complete in- and outpatient behavioral health services. Everything from around-the-clock assessments to home healthcare to ongoing support groups for individuals recovering from mood disorders, substance abuse, eating disorders, divorce, and other life-changing situations is available.

Our staff individually tailors our in- and/or outpatient services to best meet each patients needs. In addition, Linden Oaks' programs are designed to address individuals of all ages.

For more information about Linden Oaks Hospital services or for a free confidential assessment, call (630) 305-5500.

Edward Corporate Health (ECH) helps companies turn workplace health challenges into solutions. Our physicians, case managers, and nurses are occupational health experts. Their experience enables them to create strategies that help reduce employee injury and illness.

ECH's comprehensive services include injury treatment, case management, worksite/workstation assessment, physical exams, drug testing, health screenings, and wellness programs. All of these services share one overriding objective: to keep employees healthy, safe, and on the job.

To learn more about Edward Corporate Health, call (630) 527-3827.

Health & Fitness Centers

The **Edward Health & Fitness Center** in Naperville (EHFC) is a medically-based, state-of-the-art fitness facility. The 57,000-square-foot Center is located on the Edward Hospital campus, and was the first of its kind to open in DuPage County. EHFC members take advantage of the very latest cardiovascular and strength training equipment — including a running track, basketball court, and lap pool — in an environment that supports safe and effective physiologic enhancement.

Upon sign-up, each member undergoes a thorough fitness assessment which measures body fat, cardiovascular endurance, strength, and flexibility. From this starting point, each member receives a tailored fitness program from one of our staff exercise physiologists. These incorporate exercise, nutrition, and health awareness into strategies that suit each member's personal fitness goals and needs.

A second EHFC is scheduled to open in Woodridge's Seven Bridges community in the fall of 1997. This location will feature the same adult fitness amenities as the Naperville Center as well as unique children's programming that includes a youth swimming pool, fun-n-fit activities, and separate children's locker rooms.

The EHFC/Naperville is open seven days a week. If you'd like to learn about membership at our Naperville or Seven Bridges locations call (630) 717-0500.

Through ongoing fundraising efforts, the **Edward Foundation** helps enhance the quality and breadth of Edward Health Services Corporation programs and services.

Since 1990, the Edward Foundation has raised approximately $3.5 million. These funds have been applied to the acquisition of lifesaving technologies and the development of innovative programs, such as the Care Center — a diagnostic center for sexually abused children — and the Breast Cancer Rehabilitation Program, which helps women prepare for and recover from breast surgery. Generous community support and the dedication of dozens of volunteers help the Foundation fulfill its mission year after year.

To learn more about the Edward Foundation, or for contribution information, call (630) 527-3918.

Edward Health Services Corporation
801 South Washington Street
Naperville, Illinois 60540
(630) 355-0450

CENTRAL DUPAGE HEALTH SYSTEM

Central DuPage Hospital (CDH) is the core of Central DuPage Health System (CDHS). A unique network of healthcare providers and physicians, CDHS offers preventive, diagnostic, treatment, rehabilitation and skilled nursing care throughout DuPage County. Central DuPage Hospital's medical staff has over 600 physicians in more than over 40 different specialty areas. Facilities and services include: **Central DuPage Hospital,** 25 North Winfield Rd., Winfield (630) 682-1600. **For Class Registration and Physician Referral** (630) 260-2685.

Hospital specialty areas include: **Cardiology**-offering a complete, advanced heart program from prevention to treatment and rehabilitation with heart surgeons from major Chicagoland teaching hospitals. Also offered are extensive nutrition and education programs and advanced treatments such as minimally invasive heart surgery.

Obstetrics & Gynecology-offering complete care for women and infants with a complimentary nurse home visitation program for new parents and the most comprehensive Neonatal Intensive Care Unit in DuPage County. The CDH Mother/Baby Unit is also responsible for delivering the most babies in DuPage County-creating the highest number of happy families!

Surgery (and Minimally Invasive Surgery)-offering surgical expertise in all major areas including: general, cardiac, gynecologic, neurologic, orthopaedic, plastic/reconstructive, urologic, chest and ear, nose and throat. CDH physicians are leaders, in the utilization of the technique of minimally invasive or -"bandaid" surgery. Performing over 17,000 surgeries annually, CDH physicians and clinical staff handle the highest volume of procedures in DuPage County.

Orthopaedics-Orthopaedic surgeons and clinicians at CDH perform over 500 total joint (hip and knee) replacements every year. CDH is recognized as the number one facility in Illinois for patient outcomes and volumes in these surgeries!

Neurology-offering the latest in diagnostic and treatment methods such as a Stealth Station-an advanced image-guided surgery system to aid in cranial and spinal surgeries. This system, the only one in DuPage County, builds a 3D image of the patient's head and allows surgeons to perform delicate procedures with smaller incisions.

NeuroSpine-offering the latest in back surgery-laparoscopic spinal fusion (a minimally invasive technique), the NeuroSpine Unit is the premier facility in the area handling traumatic spine injuries and related surgeries.

Pediatrics/Pediatric Intensive Care-offering the most extensive pediatric services in DuPage County, with over 50 pediatricians and specialists on staff, including comprehensive Pediatric and Pediatric Intensive Care Units, CDH's children's facilities make

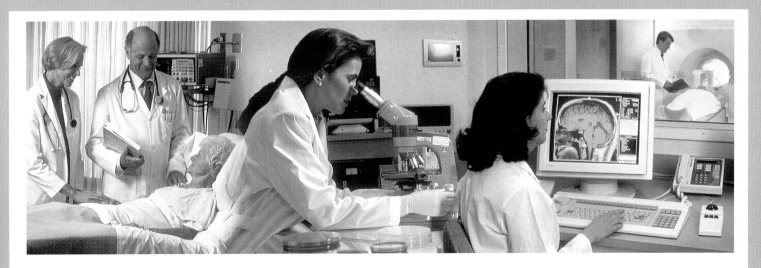

it easy for parents to be a part of the healing process.

Convenient Care Centers (630) 260-2685 (Call for exact locations). Convenient Care is medical help for minor illnesses or injuries. CDH Convenient Care Centers offer medical treatment with on-site laboratory, X-ray and mammography. Centers are open early and late, plus on holidays- no appointments necessary. There are four convenient locations- Wheaton, Bloomingdale, Naperville and St. Charles.

CENTRA Corporate Office: 27W353 Jewell Rd. Winfield, (630) 752- 8800. A primary care physician organization, CENTRA provides high- quality, accessible family healthcare to many communities in DuPage County. The physician practices in CENTRA offer a variety of convenient hours and locations and include the areas of family practice, internal medicine, obstetrics and gynecology and pediatrics.

CNS DuPage 690 E. North Ave., Carol Stream (630) 665-7000. CNS DuPage delivers affordable, compassionate home health care and hospice services to residents of DuPage,

Kane, Will, Eastern Cook and Lake Counties. This comprehensive home health agency delivers over 80,000 home visits annually to patients who require continued care following surgeries, illnesses or injuries.

Wynscape Nursing and Reha- bilitation Center 2180 W. Manchester Road, Wheaton (630) 665-4330. Whether an individual requires short-term care for respite, convalescence, rehabilitation, or hospice, Wynscape, a 209-bed unit, offers a variety of services to meet those needs. Long-term care is available for those un- able to return home.

Wyndemere Retirement Community 200 Wyndemere Circle, Wheaton (630) 690-8889. A complete lifecare retirement community, Wyndemere offers a choice of well- appointed apartment homes and townhomes for those 62 years of age and older. Wyndemere residents enjoy a worry-free lifestyle in an environment that guarantees continued quality healthcare-no matter what the need.

HealthTrack Sports & Wellness 875 Roosevelt Road, Glen Ellyn 1-888- FIT-4-EVER. Opening Fall of 1997, the HealthTrack Sports & Wellness facility

is a place to get fit and be pampered. This fitness facility is 100,000 square feet of superior health and fitness amenities including: a lap pool, warm water therapy pool, two whirlpools, full-court gymnasium, a running track, cardio fitness equipment and personal trainers. Call and get on the TRACK!

The Association For Business Health Corporate Office: 245 S. Gary Avenue Bloomingdale (630) 894-8404. Focusing on the special health needs of area businesses, ABH offers a full-range of cost-effective business health services. These include executive and post-offer physicals; health, immunization and wellness programs; back evaluations; drug testing; and work-related injury treatment and management.

Central DuPage Hospital and Health System providers-Bringing Healthcare Together For You!

For more information, visit our website at: http://www.cdh.org

Central DuPage Hospital
25 N. Winfield Road
Winfield, Illinois 60190
(630) 682-1600

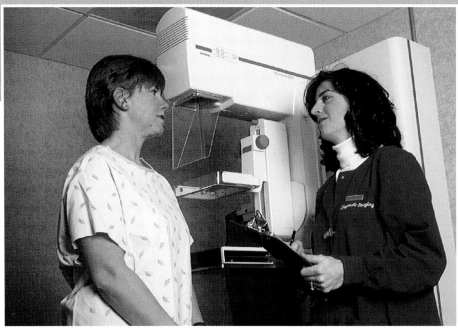

The full service capabilities of Glen Ellyn Clinic allow a patient to schedule a mammogram...

GLEN ELLYN CLINIC

Glen Ellyn Clinic is an important provider of medical services to residents of Naperville and surrounding communities. Its doctors integrate the best of new technological treatments with proven traditional methods to provide patients with high-quality, cost-effective medical care.

Established in Glen Ellyn in 1964, the clinic has served families at two Naperville locations since the 1980s — at the Edward Physician Center on Spalding Drive and at the Mill Street Medical Center, just north of Ogden Avenue.

With steady growth that parallels that of DuPage County, Glen Ellyn Clinic now offers patients the collective medical expertise and experience of more than ninety respected physicians. Representing over twenty specialty areas covering: internal medicine; family practice; allergy; audiology; cardiology; dermatology; diagnostic imaging; ear, nose and throat; gastroenterology;

laboratory services; neurology; nutrition counseling; obstetrics and gynecology; oncology; orthopaedics; pediatrics; neonatology; plastic and reconstructive surgery; physical therapy; surgery; urgent care; and urology, these doctors offer comprehensive care for every member of the family. In addition to these services, the orthopaedic doctors are official team physicians for all major athletic teams at North Central College and often provide sports medicine services at local high school games.

Glen Ellyn Clinic strives to make seeking treatment as easy and convenient as possible. With multiple sites throughout the area, its clinics are only minutes away from local homes and offices. The clinics are able to provide "one-stop" care for most families by providing numerous medical specialties under one roof. Patients are easily referred to various specialists, if needed, while remaining in the same familiar

setting. Evening and Saturday office hours make the clinic's services even more convenient and accessible.

Glen Ellyn Clinic, one of the largest managed-care entities in DuPage County, provides service to all the major HMO, POS, and PPO plans in the area, as well as Medicare and most individual and commercial employer health insurance plans. As a courtesy, Glen Ellyn Clinic automatically files with insurance companies when patients supply the necessary information.

The clinic is also teamed with MedPartners Physicians Services, Inc., part of the largest Physician Practice Management firm in the country. Through this partnership, MedPartners manages operations and handles growth, allowing Glen Ellyn Clinic to do what it does best — provide excellent doctoring to the individuals in its care.

Friendly, personalized service is the hallmark of Glen Ellyn Clinic, and the patient is the main concern of its

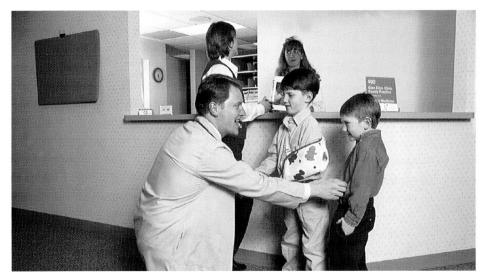
...the same day her child is seeing their family practitioner...

doctors, nurses, and staff. One example of this concern is the clinic's important Diabetes Education Center, the first of its kind in the western suburbs.

In the mid-1980s, the medical staff recognized the need for a team approach in the treatment of diabetes. Children with Type I or juvenile diabetes had a difficult time keeping track of their blood sugar levels at school and were often frightened and endangered when emergencies occurred. A team of doctors, nurses, and dieticians began to work with the children, their parents, grandparents, teachers, principals, and school nurses. By teaching each of them the symptoms and treatments of low blood sugar and how to use a blood glucose monitoring meter, Glen Ellyn Clinic experts were able to put together a strong support system to provide immediate assistance to the children and their families. The Diabetes Education Center is located at the main Glen Ellyn Clinic in Glen Ellyn. Any individual, doctor, or hospital can utilize its services.

Recognizing the need for specialized women's care, the diagnostic imaging department of the Spalding facility has installed a state-of-the-art Sieman's mammography unit. Glen Ellyn Clinic provides mammogram services at three of its facilities, all of which offer evening scheduling. Each location is fully accredited by the American College of Radiology and follows the strict guidelines of the Mammography Quality Assurance Act. In addition, the clinic requires each technician to pass a two year radiology and mammography certification course offered by the American Registry of Radiologists.

In all aspects of care, Glen Ellyn Clinic continually works to enhance its service. The clinic recently installed an EPIC computer system

that centralizes scheduling, providing faster patient access to appropriate doctors. While maintaining the highest levels of confidentiality and security, the system will also enable doctors to instantaneously access and share vital information regarding the diagnosis and treatment of individual patients.

Although there is never a "good" time to be in need of medical attention, Glen Ellyn Clinic makes seeking treatment as easy and convenient as possible. The clinic offers personalized, quality care as a well-established member of the Naperville community.

Glen Ellyn Clinic
A Commitment to Caring

Edward Physician Center
100 Spalding Drive
Naperville, 60540
(630) 355-8000
and
Mill Street Medical Center
1250 North Mill Street
Naperville, 60563
(630) 961-4161 OB/GYN
(630) 961-4166 Pediatrics

...offering them more quality time together at home.

COPLEY MEMORIAL HOSPITAL

We promise you something extraordinary.

The Copley Memorial Hospital team promise extraordinary service to you each day...a warm friendly greeting, the offer of an escort around our beautiful new hospital, comprehensive and timely information, opportunity to participate in your health care, answering call lights immediately, respecting your privacy, a sparkling clean environment, healthy tastefully prepared food, and absolutely everything possible to ensure comfort and please you!

The Copley team — physicians, employees, volunteers — make it possible for Copley Memorial Hospital to promise extraordinary service in all healthcare areas:

Cancer Care Center
Emergency Center
Extended Care Center
Home health
Intensive care/intermediate care
Medical/surgical care
Neonatology
Occupational health
Pediatrics
Physical Rehabilitation Center
Retina Center
Rush-Copley Center for Reproductive
    Health
Rush-Copley Heart Institute
Surgery Center
Tests, treatments
Wellness classes
Women's Health Center/ob-gyne
and much more!

Unique link to the Rush System for Health

Since 1987, Copley has been a member of the Rush System for Health, a network of several hospitals in the Chicago area including Rush-Presbyterian-St. Luke's Medical Center, one of the nation's leading academic healthcare, teaching, and research institutions. The affiliation provides a link to new treatments, cutting edge technology and research focused on improving patient care — all rare for a community hospital setting. And a family practice residency, offered at Copley, further enhances the environment for research and teaching.

Convenient location to Naperville

The 142-bed (all private rooms!) full service Copley Memorial Hospital moved to its present location on Ogden, just four miles west of Route 59 in November 1995. The hospital is situated on the beautiful 98-acre Rush-Copley Medical Center campus. Other campus sites are:
• Physician offices for many of our 300+

physicians practicing in 47 different specialties and subspecialties.
• Rush-Copley Healthplex, an exciting fitness and athletic center open to the community.
• Waubonsee Center at Copley an extension site of Waubonsee Community College.
• Children's World Learning Center, a child care facility.

Fast Track ER service — something good to know

Copley offers Fast Track ER service for treatment of minor illnesses and injuries. The service is designed so patients can be seen by a physician and treated and released within one hour.

Experience extraordinary service

Experience the feeling of extraordinary service. Call today for a tour, physician referral, list of our many insurance plans, or information about Copley, **(630) 978-6700.**

Rush-Copley Medical Center
Copley Memorial Hospital
2000 Ogden Avenue
Aurora, Illinois 60504
(630) 978-6200 (Main Number)
(630) 978-6700 (Physician Referral
and Information)

Saint Joseph Medical Center's Family Health Center, 24024 W. Brancaster Drive, Naperville.

SAINT JOSEPH MEDICAL CENTER

Saint Joseph Medical Center is a leading provider of high quality, state-of-the-art care to the Will County region. What began in 1882 as a 20-bed hospital in Joliet has evolved into a 542-bed regional referral center which is the flagship provider of the Franciscan Sisters Health Care Corporation.

In 1997, the Medical Center opened Project Renewal, a 90,000 sq. ft. addition and 70,000 sq. ft. renovation that brought new and enhanced services including Family Birthing Suites, allowing women to experience the miracle of birth in one comfortable setting. The unit includes a Level II nursery and round-the-clock neonatal intensive coverage. Other enhanced services include new state-of-the-art surgical suites and expanded emergency trauma services.

Will County's leader in the provision of full-service cardiac care, Saint Joseph Medical Center offers the region's first and only open heart surgery and angioplasty programs.

Saint Joseph Medical Center provides the area's most comprehensive rehabilitation services including Physical Medicine and Rehabilitation, the first inpatient rehabilitation program of its kind; the inpatient Continuing Care unit; the outpatient Physical Rehab and Sports Injury Center, that offers aquatic therapy; and the outpatient Industrial Rehabilitation Center for injured workers.

Recent additions to the list of sophisticated offerings are the region's only Sleep Disorder Center and Retina Center, a Pediatric Intensive Care unit so critically ill children can receive care close to home, the Breast Health Center and the Osteoporosis Prevention and Treatment Program.

Saint Joseph Medical Center offers Ask-A-Nurse, a 24-hour health information line staffed by registered nurses. The service, 815-725-9400, also provides physician referrals.

Saint Joseph Medical Center brought this top-notch care to Naperville in 1994 with the opening of the Family Health Center, 24024 W. Brancaster, located in the Tamarack Fairways subdivision. The Family Health Center offers a complete range of primary and specialty care physician specialists as well as lab, x-ray, mammography, family counseling and free educational seminars. Hours of operation are Mondays and Wednesdays, 8 a.m. to 7 p.m., Tuesdays and Thursdays, 8 a.m. to 8 p.m., Fridays, 8 a.m. to 5 p.m. and Saturdays, 9 a.m. to noon. The Family Health Center can be reached at (630) 904-1220.

Saint Joseph Medical Center
333 N. Madison Street
Joliet, Illinois 60435
(815) 725-7133

EDUCATION

NORTH CENTRAL COLLEGE
NAPERVILLE'S COLLEGE SINCE 1870

It is impossible to imagine Naperville without North Central College — and vice-versa.

In 1870, when the citizens of Naperville pledged the funds to build "Old Main" and attract a nine-year-old college from nearby Plainfield, they knew something: For Naperville to become a great city, it needed a great college. For more than a century and a quarter, North Central has been that institution.

The College's success in combining liberal arts education with pre-professional training, and an emphasis on inculcating leadership, ethics and values, have earned it top ranking for general excellence as one of "America's Best Colleges" by the editors of *U.S. News & World Report*, a distinction it shared in the 1990s with only two other institutions of higher education in the greater Chicago area — Northwestern and the University of Chicago.

At North Central today, more than 2,600 students enjoy the same friendly but rigorous approach to learning — small classes taught by full-time professors (one for every 14 students) and emphasis on writing and reasoning skills — that shaped alumni like James Nichols, who bequeathed Naperville its

public library system; Peter Edward Kroehler, whose Kroehler Manufacturing Company was Naperville's largest employer for three generations; Harold White, owner and publisher of the *Naperville Sun* for 50 years; Harold Moser, "Mr. Naperville," who developed most of the residential subdivisions that have become modern Naperville; and Harvey Mehlhouse, who brought Bell Laboratories to the city in the 1960s.

At the same time, with over 50 undergraduate majors; national champion track and cross country programs; a nationally-recognized college and community radio station (WONC- 89.1 FM); master's degree offerings in business, computer science and other areas; a new campus-wide voice, video and data communication network with Internet access; strong faculty in business, computer science and other fields who regularly consult with area businesses; and a wide variety of scheduling formats to accommodate students who work part-time or full-time ... North Central provides many of the benefits of a major university, but without the hassles.

From its earliest years, North Central has been a cultural gathering

place for Naperville. Since Pfeiffer Hall was built in 1926, Naperville and College residents alike have flocked to its beautiful (and recently renovated) 1,050-seat auditorium, that serves as the community's performing arts center, to enjoy countless concerts, plays, recitals and speeches by some of America's most notable intellectual and civic leaders.

As the new millennium approaches, North Central is restoring historic Old Main to its former grandeur and enjoying record enrollments. It is also preparing to build new football and baseball stadiums and a new track, and seeking support for a Fine Arts Center — all to serve both the College and the community.

North Central greets the challenges of the 21st century as a good neighbor, committed to maintaining and enhancing the quality of life which makes Naperville the envy of so many other communities.

North Central College
30 North Brainard Street
Naperville, Illinois 60566
(630) 637-5300
(800) 611-1861

BENEDICTINE UNIVERSITY

Benedictine University was founded by the Benedictine monks of St. Procopius Abbey in 1887. Originally named St. Procopius, the college began as an all-male school on the near west side of Chicago and moved to its present location in 1901. It became coeducational in 1968 and was renamed Illinois Benedictine in 1971. On April 19, 1996, Illinois Benedictine College officially changed its name to Benedictine University, reflecting the institution's full range of programs and expanding international opportunities. "Our name change to Benedictine University," said president William Carroll, "will serve as a building permit for the small, model university of the 21st Century."

The University's 108-acre campus features a comprehensive science facility, library, administrative building, four residence halls, a modern athletic center and a student center. The Scholl Science Center houses nationally recognized programs in which students gain access to the best medical and science schools in the country.

In addition to the natural sciences, Benedictine offers undergraduate majors in education, arts and humanities and social sciences, including business. Also in the mix are interdisciplinary programs in International Business and Economics and International Studies, both based on the idea that cultures interact with politics and economics/business.

Special accelerated and evening formats through the Center for Adult Learning have been developed to meet the needs of working adults. The Center was developed to provide an environment for learning which supports adults in taking responsibility for their own learning and which values and utilizes the experience an adult brings to the classroom.

Master's degrees are offered in business administration, management and organizational behavior, public health, exercise physiology, counseling psychology, fitness management, management information systems and education, as well as a Ph.D. program in organization development. The broad variety of programs in business and healthcare management provide the most comprehensive offerings in the Western suburbs. The Management and Organizational Behavior program is ranked in the top six programs nationally.

Benedictine also features a competitive intercollegiate athletic program for both men and women. "Our mission is centered around a commitment to learning," said Carroll. "We strive to prepare our students to live active, responsible and prosperous lives in the world community."

Benedictine University
5700 College Road
Lisle, Illinois 60532
(630) 829-6000

COLLEGE OF DUPAGE

College of DuPage, which first opened its doors in 1967, has taken root throughout Community College District 502 like a giant sequoia, offering myriad educational and cultural opportunities for 875,000 district residents.

The college's convenient Naperville Center is a perfect example. Located at 1223 Rickert Drive in Naperville, 942-4700, the neighborhood center offers a comprehensive selection of college-level credit courses that are applicable to the college's five associate's degrees and numerous certificate programs.

The center's diverse curriculum enables students to obtain courses delivered in a traditional classroom structure or in a schedule-friendly flexible learning format, which enables busy adults to work at their own pace. "Hands-on" instruction in a variety of Computer and Office Careers courses is provided on IBM personal computers, and English As A Second Language classes are offered in beginning, intermediate and advanced levels.

Designed to serve the lifelong learning needs of Naperville area residents is a variety of challenging and exciting non-credit courses and workshops for kids, teens and adults. Classes, programs and services are offered seven days a week.

Naperville citizens are taking full advantage of the educational opportunities. For the past 12 years, Naperville ranks first among 50 communities served by the college with more than 4,000 students enrolling for classes each quarter at the college's Glen Ellyn campus or the Naperville Center. C.O.D. ranks as the nation's largest single-campus community college serving 34,000 students.

Also branching throughout the district is the college's Business and Professional Institute, which each year assists 25,000 individuals and 2,000 small- and medium-sized businesses.

Two key areas of BPI are its Small Business Development Center (SBDC) and International Trade Center. The SBDC provides managerial, technical and general business support to the business community, while the International Trade Center counsels businesses that are exploring the international marketplace for the first time.

BPI is a major resource in the economic development of the district. For example, the institute provides non-credit and credit training at company work sites that strengthens work forces, increases managerial effectiveness, enhances productivity and improves profitability.

C.O.D. is often described by area residents as a "community jewel." With 43 pre-baccalaureate and 44 occupational/technical programs for students seeking transfer, job skills training and personal enrichment, C.O.D. reaches out to provide an educational and cultural value that will last a lifetime.

Visit C.O.D. on its home page: http://www.cod.edu.

College of DuPage
425 22nd Street
Glen Ellyn, Illinois 60137-6599
(630) 942-2380

DEPAUL UNIVERSITY

Call it a university for a metropolis. And call DePaul Naperville part of the solution to one of the tougher problems in higher education in the last quarter of century.

The problem is how to make a university meet the needs of its community when that community is undergoing unparalleled change and growth.

The center no longer holds. Commuting is now from suburb to downtown, from city to suburb and edge city, from one edge city to another. The metropolis is no longer a city with a collar of suburbs. When half the corporate headquarters are in what was called the collar, then what defines the center? And when half the students are adults, living and working with ever-more complicated schedules, what should a university look like?

It should look like DePaul. The times call for new ways of thinking and DePaul began thinking in new ways over 25 years ago when it opened the School for the New Learning, the first competency-based adult degree program in the midwest, and followed it with the first suburban campus near O'Hare. The vision was for a university that kept pace with its community.

Today, that vision has resulted in a multi-campus network, linking the population centers of a great metropolis to a great university education.

DePaul Naperville is dedicated to adult learners, with undergraduate and graduate programs in the School for New Learning — now a national model for educating working professionals — alongside MBAs from the Kellstadt Graduate School of Business (ranked sixth in the nation by *U.S. News and World Report*), a master's degree in Management of Public Services, and graduate degrees from the largest School of Computer Science, Telecommunications & Information Systems in the country, and more.

Come see the future: 60,000 square feet of campus in Naperville at 150 W. Warrenville Road — two miles west of the I-88 exit at Naperville Road. Twenty-one classrooms, state of the art video delivery systems and PC labs, resident faculty, library, bookstore, adult student services — all in service to a community.

Call it a university for the way we live now.

DePaul University - Naperville Campus
150 W. Warrenville Road
Naperville, Illinois 60563-8460
(312) 362-6500
(630) 548-9378

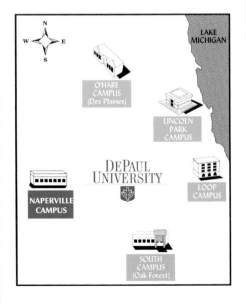

George Pradel, Mayor of the City of Naperville, is one of many volunteers who visit schools in Districts 203 and 204 to share information and expertise with students, to read with them and to tutor and mentor individual or small groups of pupils.

NAPERVILLE'S SCHOOL DISTRICTS

The city of Naperville is served by two school districts, both highly regarded large unit districts serving grades kindergarten through 12 and individuals with special needs ages 3-21 in western DuPage and northern Will counties. Naperville Community Unit School District 203 serves the older portions of Naperville, plus segments of the Village of Lisle to the east and single subdivisions within Bolingbrook and Woodridge. Indian Prairie Community Unit School District 204 serves the newer portions of Naperville, established as the city extended its boundaries to the west and southwest, and portions of Aurora and Bolingbrook.

Enrollment within District 203 is approximately 18,200 pupils within 14 elementary schools (K-5), five junior highs (6-8) and two high schools (9-12). A period of rapid growth that began after WWII has now slowed to about 1% a year and should taper off entirely within 5 years. Enrollment within District 204 should soon surpass that of District 203, which currently is the fourth largest district in Illinois. District 204 has more than 16,000 pupils within 14 elementary schools (K-5), three middle schools (6-8) and one high school (9-12). It is the fastest-growing district in Illinois and currently is constructing a second high school, a fourth middle school and a 15th elementary school — all to open in 1997. Plans are under way for six more elementaries, two more middle schools, a district educational center and additions to several existing facilities.

Both districts can boast of high-achieving students; excellent facilities, faculty and instructional programs; and the involvement of supportive parent associations, education foundations, civic and service organizations and local businesses. Students excel in athletics and the performing arts as well as in academics. Curriculum is developed on a district-wide basis in an attempt to meet the needs and learning styles of all students, ranging from handicapped to gifted. Technology is incorporated as appropriate to curriculum, with students at all levels learning computer skills and applications.

High school graduation rates and college entrance exam scores are among the state's highest. American College Test composite scores of Naperville Central and North and Waubonsie Valley students rank among the top 12 in the state.

Administrative Center
Naperville Community Unit School
District 203
203 W. Hillside Road
Naperville, Illinois 60540-6589
(630) 420-6300
Fax (630) 420-1066

QUALITY OF

LIFE

HOLIDAY INN SELECT

Holiday Inn Worldwide hand-picked this hotel to become part of its premier Holiday Inn Select line, a new group of exceptional hotels designed specifically to meet the needs and demands of the business traveler. All Holiday Inn Select hotels pamper their guests with coffee makers, irons and ironing boards, hair dryers, makeup mirrors, and well-lit desk work areas. Electronic locks, second phones with dataports, free local calls within ten miles, on-demand in-room movies, video checkout, and voice mail are additional services that are standard fare at these quality hotels. Further, all registered guests receive a complimentary *USA Today*, delivered to their room. The *"award-winning"* Holiday Inn Select Naperville has 299 guest rooms, including executive and parlor suites. Many health-conscious guests also utilize the hotel's indoor pool, fitness center, and sauna.

Numerous dining choices are available at the Holiday Inn Select —

from casual breakfast or luncheon buffets to elegant dining in the Grand Ballroom. While talking in a relaxed atmosphere under the Terrace Café's skylit atrium, guests enjoy a delicious variety of meals, fresh salad bars, and home-made desserts. The Terrace Bar, with its wide selection of micro beers, is another popular spot where business associates meet and unwind after a busy day.

Providing abundant facilities for any large event or conference, the hotel also offers 20,000 square feet of meeting space, including a 6,400 square-foot Grand Ballroom. A full-service audiovisual department furnishes equipment and expertise for a wide range of presentations, while the hotel's sales and catering department provides professional guidance to help businesses and families customize plans and menus for any occasion.

Conveniently located on Naper Boulevard, adjacent to the East-West Tollway/I-88, the Holiday Inn Select is

a short drive from many of Naperville's popular attractions, such as Naper Settlement, the Riverwalk, and the community's historic downtown. Other popular tourist destinations, such as the Morton Arboretum, Billy Graham Center, Cantigny Gardens and Museum, Oak Brook Shopping Center, Paramount Arts Center, and Hollywood Riverboat Casino are also nearby. The hotel's quick accessibility from O'Hare and Midway airports, downtown Chicago, and the northwestern suburbs via I-294 and I-355 makes it a popular choice of meeting planners and visitors alike.

Its premier location is close to major area businesses, such as AT&T Bell Labs, Lucent Technologies, Budget-Rent-A-Car, Spyglass, Allied Van Lines, Laidlaw Transit, Hewlett Packard, Millward Brown, Tellabs, General Motors, and Nike. Many of these companies make the Holiday Inn Select their first choice when arranging accommodations for their employees,

clients, and corporate guests. Many choose this hotel and conference center when planning their training seminars, conferences, and special events.

The Holiday Inn Select, Naperville's largest hotel, is an award-winning hotel and conference center that plays an important role in the commerce of this community. A local landmark, the hotel opened as the first full-service hotel in Naperville in 1981. The facility underwent a major renovation and in early 1993, the Holiday Inn Select Naperville opened its doors.

Since its inception, the Holiday Inn Select Naperville has been recognized for high levels of quality and achievement. After it's first year of operation, the hotel won Holiday Inn Worldwide's Newcomer of the Year Award, one of only 14 new Holiday Inns in the world selected for meeting the highest standards of quality and customer service. Then, in 1994, the hotel won the Torchbearer Award, the highest award presented by Holiday Inn Worldwide. Naperville's Holiday Inn Select was one of only 20 hotels in the world to receive this coveted honor. In 1995 and 1996, the hotel also received national Quality Excellence Awards, given only to hotels achieving distinction in all aspects of their operations.

The Holiday Inn Select's excellence is not limited to the customers it serves within its spacious rooms. Its excellence extends into the community as well. Recognizing the value businesses can bring to schools, service clubs, and philanthropic organizations, members of the Holiday Inn Select staff are involved in the community. The hotel is also generous in offering its services and facilities.

As Naperville continues to grow, the Holiday Inn Select has the facilities, quality, and vision to continue providing outstanding service to travelers and businesses. Management's commitment to the community also ensures that Naperville's residents and service organizations will continue to benefit from its expertise and resources.

Holiday Inn Select
1801 Naper Boulevard
Naperville, Illinois 60563
(630) 505-4900

NAPER SETTLEMENT

In 1969, when a group of visionary residents fought to save what is now Century Memorial Chapel, little could they have imagined that their efforts would result in the creation of Naper Settlement, Chicagoland's only nineteenth century living history village. Recognizing that Naperville's historic structures needed to be preserved, these volunteers founded the Naperville Heritage Society and developed a master plan that included saving significant structures and moving the buildings to the thirteen-acre site surrounding the Martin-Mitchell House.

Today, Naper Settlement is known throughout the region for its historic buildings and important educational programs. The village provides a glimpse into village life from the time Naperville was a frontier post in 1831 until it was a bustling Victorian Age community at the turn of the century.

In early 1997, Naper Settlement reached another important milestone with the grand opening of the Pre-Emption House, a replica of Naperville's first hotel and tavern, built in 1835. The original hotel welcomed travelers on the road between Chicago and Galena and once stood at the corner of what is today Chicago Avenue and Main Street. It was the site of much of the town's activity — from the "pre-empting" of parcels of land at $1.25 an acre to horse trading during outdoor market days, to grand balls attended by Chicago's finest.

Today's Pre-Emption House will again serve the region as a center of activity — and as the gateway to Naper Settlement. Outside, the building replicates the famed hotel of the 1860s. Inside, visitors can view the nineteenth-century-style lobby and men-only tavern. The remainder of the building has been modified to house the Museum

Store, gallery and exhibit space, curatorial workspace and archives, research library, classroom facilities, and the museum's administrative offices. The museum's collection of Lester Schrader paintings, depicting Naperville's early history, are on display in the building's 4,000+ square-foot gallery on the lower level.

As with so many of the places and events that enhance Naperville's quality of life, the successful re-creation of Naper Settlement and the Pre-Emption House are largely the result of time, money, and materials generously donated by the community's residents and businesses.

Naper Settlement
523 S. Webster Street
Naperville, Illinois 60540-6517

NAPERVILLE PARK DISTRICT

The Naperville Park District, with administrative offices along the Riverwalk, enjoys a national reputation as a leader in parks and recreation. Its beautiful parks, award-winning programs, and highly-acclaimed cooperative agreements offer outstanding recreational opportunities for local residents and provide excellent models for other communities.

The second largest park district in the state, the Naperville Park District owns or manages over 2,300 acres of parkland. This includes large community parks, such as the Riverwalk and DuPage River Park, smaller neighborhood parks, and a variety of natural areas. As a separate unit of government, the park district works in close cooperation with the City of Naperville and the Forest Preserve District of DuPage County to preserve natural areas, establish green belts, create bike trails, and provide open space and recreational areas as the community grows.

The park district also owns or leases various facilities throughout the community, including Naperbrook and Springbrook golf courses, Centennial Beach, the Alfred Rubin Riverwalk Community Center, The Barn, the Warming Shelter, and Sportsman's Park. As a result of innovative cooperative agreements with the schools, the park district also utilizes several elementary school gymnasiums when they are not scheduled for use by the schools.

The Naperville Park District offers more than 3,980 different programs each year, providing a vast array of recreational experiences for participants of all ages. From preschool programs that build youngsters' large-motor skills, to social activities for junior high students, to sports leagues for teens and adults, to exciting classes and trips for older adults, the park district offers something for everyone. Thousands of families participate in summer swimming programs, softball leagues, and other recreational programs that involve the whole family.

Each year, the park district cosponsors various community events with local service organizations. In the spring, it co-hosts an Easter Egg hunt, and summer brings the award-winning Ribfest. Named the "Best Festival in the Midwest" for more than five years, Ribfest lasts four to five days, features eighteen rib vendors, family activities, carnival games, and performances by well-known musical groups. Then, on October 31, Halloween Happening gives children and their parents a delightful opportunity to trick or treat at Naper Settlement, which park district workers temporarily transform into a magical fantasyland. The Haunted House, held at Centennial Beach Bath House, is another fall activity everyone enjoys.

Since it was established more than 30 years ago, the park district has encouraged residents to "Take Time for Fun!" Residents have responded enthusiastically, and the resulting programs, parks, and facilities have enhanced the quality of life for everyone who comes to Naperville.

Naperville Park District
320 W. Jackson Avenue
Naperville, Illinois 60540
(630) 357-9000

NAPERVILLE TOWNSHIP

Township government is one of the oldest forms of government in the United States, predating even the United States Constitution. Most township lines are drawn in a square, six miles on each side. When the country's population lived in mostly rural areas, this guaranteed that no one was more than six miles from local government. Today Illinois still has over 1,400 townships, and five of them at least partially reside in Naperville.

The most visible of these is Naperville Township, located along the Riverwalk in downtown. The township is run by four trustees and a township supervisor. Eight officials, including the trustees, supervisor, highway commissioner, assessor, and township clerk, are elected every four years. They meet publicly twice each month. The second Tuesday in April, all townships in the state have an "old fashioned town meeting," reminiscent of pioneering days.

The role of Naperville Township, like other townships, is unique. All the commercial and residential assessments within the township's borders are conducted by the assessor's office. The assessor's office also assists residents with real estate tax exemptions. The highway commissioner, as the elected official in charge of the township road district, is responsible for maintaining all streets and roads in unincorporated areas and working cooperatively with other units of government to guarantee efficiency. The town clerk is the "keeper" of the official seal and maintains public records according to law. The clerk also coordinates voter registration at the township office. The township supervisor is treasurer of all town and road district funds, as well as administrator of senior services and various general assistance and emergency assistance programs.

If people are not eligible for public aid, they are automatically considered for general assistance programs in times of need. When facing life-threatening situations, such as evictions, people can turn to the township to help them. Applications can be made quickly and effectively.

Naperville Township has an extremely active program for senior citizens. Working in cooperation with local police and sheriff's departments, the township offers TRIAD, a program to educate older citizens about crimes that affect them. Naperville Township also supports transportation for the elderly, Senior Home Sharing, and Ecumenical Adult Day Care.

Required to have a program for youth, Naperville Township provides funds to NCO Youth and Family Services to support counseling and an emergency shelter for young people. Naperville Township also supports holiday food baskets, low-income legal assistance for qualified residents, and other services.

Naperville Township
139 Water Street
Naperville, Illinois 60540-5384
(630) 355-2786

NAPERVILLE VISITORS BUREAU

The Naperville Visitors Bureau acts as the host of Naperville, ensuring that your first experience here makes you likely to return. With over 14 choices of accommodations and more than 160 restaurants in the community, the bureau is a valuable source of information. Brimming with resources and an intricate network of contacts, it offers "one-stop shopping" for any person or group planning a trip to this destination city.

With a thorough knowledge of the area's hotels and conference centers, the Visitors Bureau can quickly help businesses sort through abundant choices to select meeting sites that fulfill their needs — from room accommodations, to auditoriums and break-out rooms, to audiovisual capabilities. The Visitors Bureau can also obtain special rates for groups by going out to bid with individual specifications. Providing the names of local printers, florists, and caterers is another service the Visitors Bureau offers to assist with meeting planning.

Bus tour leaders and other travelers often call on the Visitors Bureau to provide itineraries, a list of local attractions, including historic Naper Settlement, and information about community extravaganzas, such as Ribfest, the Last Fling, Oktoberfest, the Grand Prix, and other annual events. The bureau also provides information about shopping, nightlife, the Riverwalk, and customized tours on the Naperville Trolley. In addition, the Naperville Visitors Bureau helps callers find accommodations, ranging from a charming bed and breakfast within walking distance of downtown to large hotels with elegant dining rooms and fitness centers.

Also popular is the restaurant guide published by the Restaurant Council. The booklet highlights more than 60 local restaurants and includes menus and prices. Visitors can quickly find the perfect cafe or dining establishment to suit their tastes, budgets, or special gatherings.

Dedicated to making Naperville a pleasant and easily accessible destination, the Naperville Visitors Bureau streamlines the process groups often follow to bring events to this community. For example, when the Danskin National Woman's Triathlon approached Naperville about becoming a site for their annual event, the Visitors Bureau quickly arranged a meeting with the officials necessary to make the proposal a reality. In addition, the director of tourism arranged site inspections, gathered potential sponsors, kept potential participants informed, and helped educate the local business community about the economic benefits of attracting such an event. By expediting the entire process, the Naperville Visitors Bureau was instrumental in bringing this prestigious national event to Naperville.

Whether working with individuals or large groups, the Naperville Visitors Bureau offers the same level of resources and assistance to all of this community's guests.

Naperville Visitors Bureau
131 W. Jefferson Avenue
Naperville, Illinois 60540
1 (800) 642-STAY

REFERENCES:

Central District Urban Design Plan: Naperville, Summary Report, Brown/Heldt Associates, San Francisco, July 1974.

Historic Naperville, Genevieve Towsley, November 1975, The Naperville Sun, Inc.

Naperville Area Handbook and Guide, Jini Leeds Clare and Janet Reed, Naperville, 1997.

North Central College and Naperville, A Shared History: 1870-1995, Ann Durkin Keating and Pierre Lebeau, North Central College, 1995.

Our Town in Illinois, The Naperville Sun, Illinois Sesquicentennial Section, 1968.

The Phoenix Land, The Natural History of DuPage County, Wayne Lampa, Forest Preserve District of DuPage County.

Prelude to Disaster: The Course of Indian-White Relations which Led to the Black Hawk War of 1832, Anthony F. C. Wallace, Illinois State Historical Library, Springfield, 1970.

This is Naperville, "The Early History of Naperville," Genevieve Towsley, *The Naperville Sun,* Naperville, Illinois, 1975.

We Are Family: History of the Pre-Emption House and The Gertrude Hiltenbrand-Wehrli Family, Joyce Elizabeth Wehrli, Naperville, Illinois, 1993.

RESOURCES:

Carl Alston, Naperville Park District

Phoebe Bickhaus, Naperville Community Unit School District 203

Brand Bobosky, Community Volunteer

Penny Catour, Indian Prairie Community Unit School District 204

Peggy Frank, Naper Settlement

Debbie Grinnell, Naper Settlement

Steven P. Hyett, Naperville Historian

Gary Karafiat, City of Naperville

Jo Lundeen, Photos by Jo

Julie McCutcheon, CANDO

Brook McDonald, Conservation Foundation of DuPage County

Naperville Heritage Society

Cindy Pepple, Naperville Visitors Bureau

Jeana Rettig, Edward Hospital

Les Schrader, Naperville Historical Artist

Mike Skarr, Naperville Area Chamber of Commerce

Leon Toussaint, Naperville Historian

Mary-Claire Uselding, North Central College

Kim Weeks, Naperville Area Chamber of Commerce

Donna Wyman, Naper Settlement

INDEX

150

CORPORATE PROFILES IN EXCELLENCE INDEX